OUR MONEY

How to shrink government,
boost business, eliminate poverty,
and make the economy work properly
for everyone.

By

Malcolm Henry

Published by QEI Projects Ltd 2013

Text copyright © Malcolm Henry 2012
All rights reserved

ISBN: 978-0-9926285-1-2

Foreword

This started out as a project to find out how money and credit work but it has grown into something much more interesting. It appears that money is just about the cleverest thing that humankind has ever invented but we have been using it in just about the stupidest way possible. This book is an attempt to explain what money is and how we could use it to make our economy work much better for the benefit of everyone. I've spent the last 30 years as a self-employed foot-soldier engaged in the daily struggle to keep cash flowing in sufficient quantity through a variety of businesses, and have tackled the subject of our economy from this perspective. Yes, it's a book about economics but it's been written by someone who has tried and failed to understand economic textbooks and habitually nods off when reading the finance pages in the newspaper. I've aimed the book at the ordinary punter who's trying to make sense of an economic system that's patently dysfunctional. If it gets a bit technical in places please forgive me (it's a complex subject) and plough on through until the fog clears. I promise it will be worth the effort.

Contents

Introduction	1
1 | Nonsense	6
2 | Money	16
3 | Economy	34
4 | Dysfunction	53
5 | Function	71
6 | Five Things	86
7 | Common Cashflow Fund	101
8 | Payback Effects	109
9 | Bank Reform	122
10 | Workforce	137
11 | Government	146
12 | Our Money	162
References	168

Introduction

Living in the UK in the second decade of the 21st century makes me one of the most fortunate souls in the history of humankind. The supermarkets are stuffed full with food that has been brought from near and far to satisfy my appetite whenever I feel a bit peckish. My house is spacious and comfortable, warm in winter and cool in summer. I can travel where I want whenever I want thanks to my car, a reliable supply of fuel and a network of well-maintained roads that extends to every corner of the country. I can communicate with friends and colleagues around the world via internet and telephone, and enjoy the fruits of a million creative minds through digital music, film, and television. All of this is available to me for as long as I have money to pay for it. That is the thing: living in the UK in the second decade of the 21st century ***with money to spend*** makes me one of the most fortunate souls in the history of humankind. Without enough money to keep it rolling along, my life of comfort, security and opportunity will very quickly disintegrate and I will be just another participant in the misery of human poverty that stretches back as far as time itself. In recent centuries some efforts have been made by governments and charities to prevent the worst effects of poverty by taking some money from the rich and giving it to the poor so that they are able to buy food and shelter, but even in a land as wealthy as the UK some people still go to bed hungry and cold because they don't have enough money to buy food and fuel. This is absolute poverty and it serves as a warning to the rest of us: if you don't get hold of enough money every week to pay your bills the cold and unforgiving arms of penury are waiting to gather you in. We get the money that we need from a variety of sources – wages and salaries, loans, investments, pensions, welfare benefits – all of which are affected in some way by the performance of the economy. In the good times when business is booming money is relatively easy to get hold of because jobs are plentiful, banks are keen to lend, dividends are healthy and if the government of the day is feeling benevolent it makes sure that welfare benefits are generous enough to keep the wolf from most people's doors. But the good times never last. When the bad times come along more people experience the hard reality of not having enough money to buy the things that they need, and the rest of us are given a stark reminder that there, but for the grace of the money god, go I. The fact that our economy lurches from good times to bad times, from boom to bust, means that the fear of poverty is with all of us all of the time. Ultimately it's this fear that drives us, pushing at our backs, spurring us on to get more money, more wealth, more stuff to wrap around us to insulate us from the nagging threat of being poor.

From an individual perspective our fear of poverty is perfectly rational: we see what it's like to be poor and we know that we don't want to end up there. But the world as a whole is a very prosperous place providing an abundance of everything that everybody needs to be well fed and comfortable. From a global perspective poverty is caused by a failure to share: if we were certain that we'd always get our fair share of what we need then we'd have no fear of going without. The problem is that we're not very good at sharing because of a combination of our fear of poverty and a tendency towards selfishness that too often develops into greed. We have, however, developed a very successful system that allows us to share everything that the world produces with everyone who needs it, which we call the global economy. No matter where you are in the world you can get whatever you need to keep yourself fed, sheltered and entertained just as long as you have money to pay for it. The problem with the system is that lots of people struggle to get hold of enough money to pay for their basic needs. Some so-called left wing economists and politicians argue that more money should be taken from people who have lots of it and given to people who don't have enough. On the other side of the debate so-called right wing economists and politicians tell us that the only way to tackle poverty is to allow businesses to flourish, which will create lots of jobs, which will spread wealth down through society so that everyone has a fair share according to their contribution. History tells us that neither approach works. Taxing the rich sounds fair to most of us until we realise that we are included in the category of people who will have to pay more tax. We never allow ourselves to be taxed enough to stop all the poor people from remaining poor. Spreading wealth to everyone when the economy flourishes sounds plausible as a theory but what actually happens is that the rich get richer and the rest of us get further into debt, while the poor stay poor.

Economists, bankers and politicians are the people who we employ to manage our economic system and they have consistently failed to provide us with one that works properly for everyone. While they argue back and forth about this or that policy and theory our economy lurches from boom to bust. The banking crisis of 2007/08 was a sharp reminder of the lack of competence of the people who are supposed to know what they're doing. The system on which we all rely for managing the flow of money through the economy came to a virtual standstill thanks to the greed and/or stupidity of the people who we trusted to keep it working on our behalf. Now these same people who allowed the banking crisis to happen are busy arguing about what might be done to reduce the chances of it happening again, but their proposed solutions involve nothing more than tinkering with component parts like bank regulation and deposit insurance. No-one in power appears to acknowledge that the entire system is dysfunctional and needs to be reformed. No-one in power appears to have the foggiest idea about how to transform our economic system so that it gives all of us access to the things that we need to sustain our lives, and creates an environment where the people who produce these things can thrive. If the so-called experts aren't capable of doing the job we must do it ourselves. The purpose of this book is to discover why our economic system is so dysfunctional and to suggest ways in which it could be reformed for the benefit of everyone. I've already pointed out that our planet is perfectly capable of providing all of us with the stuff that we need to live in comfort, and that all of this stuff is available to anyone who has enough money to buy it. Money appears to be the key, so this book is all about money: what it is, how it works, how our misuse of it condemns some of us to absolute poverty and most of the rest of us to the fear of it. The aim of the book is to explore how we can use the magic of money to make our economy work properly for everyone. I use the example of the United Kingdom but the observations and ideas can be applied to every nation that allows people to buy and sell in a more or less free market using a common currency.

1 | Nonsense

Over the course of three decades I made several attempts to learn something about economics but each time I picked up a textbook my hopes of understanding the subject withered and died. The theories that I found in the books started in places that I didn't recognise, used assumptions that didn't make sense, and led me into a maze of mathematics where I became well and truly lost. Each attempt left me feeling that I wasn't clever enough or I lacked the necessary education to come to grips with such a complex subject, so I gave up. In 2011 the eurozone crisis was big news. The airways were thick with politicians, journalists and economists, all pontificating on the nature of the crisis and what was being done to solve it. Meanwhile there were riots on the streets of Athens, governments collapsing across Europe, and a general sense of economic doom and gloom. The fall-out from the global banking crisis of 2007/08 seemed to have poisoned the economies of the western world and no-one appeared to have a clue about how to fix it. Once again, I found myself itching to understand the underlying economics that were causing all of this social turmoil and human misery. The banking crisis appeared to have been caused by a credit boom, and the euro was obviously at the heart of the eurozone crisis. So instead of reaching for another economics textbook, I decided to concentrate on trying to learn something about money and credit.

While roaming around the internet in search of enlightenment I was unsurprised to find a lot of criticism of economists – the people who are supposed to know how our economies work. What did surprise me was that much of this criticism was coming from other economists who appeared to be accusing their peers of not understanding their own subject. Intrigued by this I dug a bit deeper and discovered that what's called 'neo-classical' economics – the stuff that is taught as standard in every university across the world and learned by every professional economist who works for any government or central bank – is based on a series of ludicrous assumptions and dodgy mathematics. The reason that I couldn't make sense of the theories that I found in thirty years of standard textbooks is because they are nonsense. This orthodox view of economics sees the economy in terms of supply and demand and assumes there is a natural tendency towards equilibrium between the two, which will always lead to a balance between production and consumption and, by inference, a stable economy. The highly unstable boom and bust cycles of the last 100 years makes these assumptions of equilibrium and stability hard to swallow. It gets worse. Most neo-classical theories are based on the motivations and actions of an imaginary individual person and an imaginary individual business each of which makes perfectly rational decisions. The mathematics that are used to describe how the economy works assume that these two entities – a person and a business – always choose the options that lead to the best possible outcomes for themselves. This might be plausible for a very simple choice where identical products are offered at different prices, for example, but in the real world choices are much more complex and the effects of them in the short, medium, and long terms are impossible to work out no matter how clever you are at maths or the size of your computer. Far from being intelligent agents that calculate every buying and selling decision to maximise their advantage, individuals and businesses make decisions on habit, convenience and whim, all of which makes a nonsense of the notion of rational optimisation. And it gets even worse. When it comes to macroeconomics – the study of economies at a national or international scale – these economic theories assume that all individual people and businesses are motivated to act in exactly the same way for any given set of circumstances. Utter nonsense. If you dig into the writings of economists from John Maynard Keynes and Hyman Minsky to Steve Keen and Richard Werner you will find plenty of evidence to support my conclusion that neo-classical economics is based on fantasy and, as such, cannot help us to understand how our economy works or what we might do to make it work better. This is worrying because most of the people who are trying to lead us out of our present economic mess have all been schooled in orthodox economics. Their careers have been built on the back of this expertise and they are understandably reluctant to hold up their hands and admit that it's nothing more than a display of intellectual gymnastics that makes sense only within the economists' mental play park but is of little or no use in the real world. Some economists on the fringes of the mainstream have been challenging the orthodoxy for decades, and they're beginning to get noticed, but the debate will almost certainly rage for a long time before we see any significant shift in the current teaching or practice of economics by professional economists. In the meantime our economies continue to struggle, apparently unable to pull themselves out of the stagnant mire into which they have fallen. History suggests that we are in the bust part of a depressingly familiar cycle and, if we hunker down and hold on, the boom will surely come. But the impotence of our elected leaders and their economic advisors to control these waves of boom and bust is glaringly obvious. Conventional economics is a busted flush and establishment economists can no longer be trusted to look after the economy on our behalf. There are probably lots of good ideas and some wisdom coming from the anti-establishment rebels, but we should be wary of allowing them to lead us out of the mess because, although they may be talking sense it's difficult for the rest of us to understand what they're saying. For a century or more economists have bamboozled us with language and concepts that are comprehensible only to themselves and have used this jargon to empower their profession, making us believe that they have a monopoly on the expertise that's required to run our economies. If we allow the new wave of anti-establishment economists to replace the current theories with a new set that are equally incomprehensible then there is a danger that we will be duped once again. We need to learn how our economic system works and describe it in language that everyone can understand: only then will we be able to see what changes can be made to get the system working more effectively. Some academic economists are very clever people and they will certainly be able to help us in this endeavour, but economics is too important to be left to academics. Far from being wise prophets guiding us through the jungle of the real-world economy, economists have a track record of leading us seriously astray and therefore cannot be trusted to sort out the mess that we're in.

Like economists, bankers have built up a mystique around their profession. We are told that our bankers are the brightest and the best, and that their innovative and entrepreneurial skills are vital to the health of our economy. They tell us that regulation or reform of the banking system in the UK will force all of this talent to migrate, leaving us bereft of the taxes that they pay, condemned to economic stagnation for evermore. What we're told and what we see are very different. We see bankers who presided over the biggest collapse of the banking system since the 1930s (without the support of the taxpayer much of the UK's banking sector would have gone bust between 2007 and 2009). Far from being essential to our economy, the individuals who ran our commercial banks were major culprits, largely responsible for creating the economic crisis and the subsequent recession. As for their general contribution to the economy, we'll discover in later chapters how banks contribute to the concentrations of wealth that stifle productive activity and create the conditions for the 'bust' half of the boom-bust rollercoaster ride that has become so familiar. Now that we're bumping along, slipping in and out of recession, we see banks refusing to lend money to commercial businesses, thereby starving the economy of the money that it needs to recover its health. It is nonsense to suggest that banking as it is currently practised is essential for our economic well-being. Our existing banking system is clearly an impediment to restoring and maintaining the health of the economy. The primary purpose of banking as we know it is to make the owners and operators of the banks as rich as possible, and we'll see that this primary purpose is in direct conflict with the best interests of the rest of us. The sooner that our banking system is reformed and the charlatans who ran it into the ground fulfil their threat of plying their trade elsewhere, the better.

Unless you're an economist or a banker you're probably quite enjoying this. Well don't get too comfortable because the rest of us must shoulder our share of the blame for the mess that we're in. Few of us have taken the trouble to understand how our economic system works. We've been happy to let the so-called experts get on with it despite decades of evidence to suggest that they're as clueless as the rest of us, and we must therefore take some responsibility for the flaws in the system and the harm that they cause. When it comes to love of money, which drives the dysfunctional system, few of us are any different to the bankers and their chums. Most of us like the idea of being rich and will jump at any chance to increase our personal pile of money with little regard for the wider consequences. For example, the housing bubble that contributed so significantly to the crash of 2007 was made possible only because so many of us bought into the ludicrous idea that house prices could increase indefinitely. We agreed to take on 100% mortgages with the promise of nice fat capital gains as house prices went up and up. This desire for personal gain is also responsible for the national debt (total government borrowing) and the deficit (the annual difference between government spending and income) that has become such a focus of government policy in recent years. Of the money that each of us gets every month, we want to keep as much of it as possible for ourselves. At the same time, we demand lots of expensive things from the government and expect to get them without paying for them out of our personal pile of cash. Our desire for maximum personal gain for minimum personal expense means that the government has to borrow money to fill the gap that we're not prepared to fill from our own resources. To suggest that the problems with our economy are all someone else's fault, that we're just innocent victims, is nonsense. Our attitude to money – our desire to 'have' more of it – is a major part of the problem. If we want to make our economy work better for everyone we have to start thinking about money in a different way.

We tend to use words like 'earn' or 'make' when talking about how money comes into our possession, which implies that money is a measure of effort or worth. We respect people who 'earn' a weekly wage and look at those who 'make' lots of money with a mixture of admiration and envy. But if we look at what people 'earn' we find that there's no correlation between the amount of money that's handed over and the amount of effort that's put in on the part of the recipient. A senior executive in an insurance company can be paid £1,000/day to sit in a comfortable chair in a warm office to shuffle information about. Meanwhile his twin brother, equally well educated and able, is being paid £100/day as a deckhand on a trawler somewhere west of Shetland, catching fish. Any desk jockey who has worked on a deep-sea trawler will tell you which job requires more effort and is more worthy of reward. We need to understand that rates of pay are determined by economic geography and have nothing to do with how hard someone works. Nor do they have anything to do with the value of a person's contribution to society. Money is not a measure of worth. If we talk about 'earning' money we imply that the money was given in exchange for something worthwhile, which is not necessarily the case. One woman can be paid a million pounds a year as director of a tobacco company while another is paid a few thousand pounds for dispensing love and kindness as a care worker in a home for the elderly. Whose work is more worthwhile? As for the idea that someone is 'making money', that really is ridiculous. The phrase is typically used by entrepreneurs – 'we're making money' – when business is profitable, but they're not 'making' money, they're capturing it. When a business is profitable it means that it's getting in more money than it's spending so the surplus money piles up, that's all. As with remuneration, there is no correlation between profitability and value. Profit margins on most farm produce are tiny while the mark-up on a paper party hat can be several hundred percent. Milk and eggs sustain life while a party hat has little value during the party and none at all by the time everyone has gone home. The amount that we are willing to spend on stuff is determined by our culture, plain and simple. A handbag with the word 'Gucci' printed on it may sell for £500 while a better quality one without the magic word sells for £50. We pay what we expect to pay. The amount has nothing to do with the inherent value of the thing that we're buying. Using money as a measure of value is nonsense, and using words like 'earn' and 'make' to describe how we get hold of it is misleading. Another money word that has positive connotations is 'save'. From childhood we're taught that 'saving' money is a good thing. Later in the book we'll see how 'saving' money can cause serious damage to an economy and how our emotional response to the notion of saving is largely nonsensical. From now on you'll notice that instead of 'earn', 'make', and 'save' I tend to use words like 'get', 'capture', and 'hoard' when describing the things that we do with money because these words more accurately describe our use of money and will help us to understand how our attitude to money has to change in order to make our economy work properly.

Before we start looking at how to sort out the mess that the nonsense of economics, banking, and our attitudes to money have got us into we'd better make sure that we know what money actually is.

2 | Money

I used to have a very clear picture in my head of what my money looked like. It was all coins and notes, some of which were in my pocket and the rest were sitting in a big pile in the bank. My share of this pile of money was shown in my bank account statement. The coins and notes in my pocket could be exchanged for things that I wanted to buy, and when they ran out I could get more from my share of the pile in the bank. Money, as I understood it, was a version of barter that was more convenient than exchanging pigs for turnips. Each coin and note had a tangible value in the same way that a pig or a turnip has a tangible value. When I discovered that most of the money 'in the bank' is nothing more than numbers in a computer the picture in my head of my money became a bit blurred. It felt like I had two different types of money. Coins and notes felt like 'real' money while the numbers in the bank's computer felt like 'made up' money. Then I was told that the bank doesn't have a store of coins and notes that add up to the same amount as the balances in all of its customers' bank accounts. In fact coins and notes account for less than 3% of the money in the UK's economy, the rest is digital money – numbers in a computer. I struggled to see how these numbers on a computer screen could be thought of as money when they didn't relate to anything that I could pick up and put in my pocket.

Money, it seemed, was not as simple to understand as I'd thought. Digging a bit deeper into the subject I discovered that I wasn't alone in finding it hard to grasp the nature of money. Academics offer a variety of explanations, most of which are as clear as mud, often disagreeing on points of detail. Everyone else seemed to have as hazy an understanding as myself.

So what can we say about money that helps us to understand what it is? Academics talk of money as 'a means of exchange' and 'a store of value'. These are useful descriptions that we recognise as spending and saving, but they describe two functions of money – things that we *do* with it – they don't tell us what money actually *is*. We could use pigs or turnips as mediums of exchange or as stores of value, but we can't put a pig or a turnip into a computer, so they're definitely not money as we now know it. Academics also talk of money as 'a unit of account'. By this they mean that money is a record of what people owe to each other. I think this gets us closer to understanding what modern money actually *is*. So let's try to understand money as a unit of account – a means of recording who owes what to whom. When someone is owed something they are in credit. When someone owes something, they are in debt. Money is a system of recording these credits and debts.

The twenty pound note in my pocket is a record of account between me and the Bank of England. It means that the Bank of England owes me twenty pounds. I am £20 in credit and the Bank of England is £20 in debt. We have a perfectly balanced credit-debt relationship. When I spend the £20 note on fuel for my car the credit side of the relationship is transferred from me to the owner of the filling station, while the debt remains with the Bank of England. The £20 credit-debt relationship continues to exist but one of the parties in the relationship has changed.

When I log into my RBS bank account on the internet and see that I have a balance of £400 this is a record of account which shows that RBS owes me £400. I am £400 in credit and RBS is £400 in debt. When I use my bank card to buy new tyres for my car the £400 is transferred electronically to the garage owner's bank account at LloydsTSB. The £400 credit-debt relationship continues to exist but it's now between two new parties, the garage owner and LloydsTSB.

As far as I'm concerned the digital money in my RBS account is exactly the same stuff as the £20 note in my pocket – a record of a credit-debt relationship that I can use as payment when I want to buy stuff. The digital money is just as 'real' as the £20 note. The only difference between them is the way in which the record is kept and how it is transferred. I can hear some economists, professional and amateur, harrumphing that I've got this all wrong. They'll tell you that the £20 note is base money (M0), which is very different from the demand deposit in my bank account (M4), and then they'll bamboozle you with definitions of each of these. But in practice the £1 coin in your pocket is worth exactly the same as £1 in your bank account – both can be used to buy a pint of milk and both are nothing more than a record of a credit-debt relationship. From the perspective of the user of the money, cash and bank money are exactly the same thing.

So money, as we know it today, is not a tangible thing that we can hold in our hand or pile up in the vault of a bank. Money is not pigs or turnips or gold, nor is it notes and coins, nor does it have any inherent value. This last one is hard to understand but getting to grips with it is vitally important if we are going to make money work better for us. A £20 note has no physical value: it's just a piece of paper with some words and pictures printed on it. Of itself the £20 note is just as ephemeral as the numbers in the computer that show your bank balance. Both are nothing more than a record of a promise by the debtor to give the creditor something of similar value at some point in the future. Money is nothing more than a promise and its value is ultimately dependent on our trust in whoever is on the debtor side of the credit-debt relationship. RBS trusts the Bank of England to honour its promise to exchange the £20 note for digital money in RBS's reserve account, which means I trust RBS to exchange the £20 note for digital money in my account. Notes, coins, and numbers in a computer are, of themselves, valueless – they're just different ways of recording a promise of future exchange. The value of money lies in whatever we buy with it, not in the money itself. The reason that this ephemeral, valueless money system works is because we agree that it works. We accept records of credit as our wages and salaries, and shopkeepers agree that we can use them to buy the stuff that we need. Crucially we can use these records of credit to pay our taxes, which means the state plays a fundamental role in securing our collective agreement that money is our common currency.

Every £1 in the UK economy is a record of one unit of money that's owed to someone by someone else. How many of these units of money are there and where did they come from? The answer to the second question will help to explain the answer to the first. Most people, if asked, would probably guess that the money in the UK economy was created by the government or by the Bank of England. They would be partly right. Her Majesty's Treasury is the government department that's responsible for public finances and it owns the Royal Mint which is where all of our coins are created. The Treasury also has the ultimate right to print and issue banknotes but it has given this power to the Bank of England and, for historical reasons, seven commercial banks (three Scottish and four Irish). The Bank of England is also responsible for creating central bank reserves. These reserves are digital money (numbers in a computer) that the central bank (Bank of England) holds on account for each of the commercial banks that operate in the UK. Central bank reserves are used for transactions between individual commercial banks and also for transactions between the commercial banks and the Bank of England. All of the money that was created by the Treasury and the Bank of England – coins, notes, and central bank reserves – accounts for approximately 12% of the money in the UK economy. The remaining 88% is the digital money that everybody has in their bank account, which was created by the banks themselves. I'll repeat that just to make sure you've got it: the vast majority (c.88%) of the money in the UK economy was created, out of nothing, by privately owned profit-making commercial banks (RBS, Lloyds, Barclays, HSBC, etc.). It sounds hard to believe, but it's true. Here's how it works.

When my bank lends me £1,200 it doesn't move £1,200 from its reserves into my account. What actually happens is that someone in the bank, sitting at a computer, types a £1,200 deposit into my account and 'hey presto!' I have £1,200 which has been created out of thin air. This can be a very difficult concept to grasp because it just doesn't feel right. Does this mean that the banker sitting at the computer can create an endless supply of money? Yes, that's exactly what it means, but there's a constraint on how fast he can create it. The bank can only create new money in the form of a loan, and its customers will only borrow as much as they think they can afford to pay back (with interest). So the ability of a bank to create money is limited by its customers' ability to repay loans. I can hear more harrumphing. In theory the bank's ability to make loans is restricted by the amount of reserves that it holds at the central bank. At the end of every business day a bank has to balance its books by demonstrating that it has enough reserves to cover a certain percentage of all of the loans that it has outstanding. This might appear to be a major restriction on the banks' ability to create money but let's think what happens to the money that they create in the form of loans. If I borrow £100,000 from RBS to buy a house from someone who banks with RBS, when I make the payment for the house the money stays within the bank, so RBS doesn't have to use any reserves to account for the £100,000 loan. Let's say the person who sold the house to me uses the £100,000 to buy a house from someone who banks at HSBC. In this case the payment leaves RBS £100,000 short, but there's a good chance that on the same day another customer has taken out a £100,000 loan at HSBC and used the money to buy something from a customer at RBS. So between them RBS and HSBC have created £200,000 of new money without having to call on any of their reserves to balance their books. This means that as long as all of the big banks are making loans at a similar rate, and most of the borrowers are spending the money, the banks can create as much money as they like without paying much attention to the reserve requirements of the Bank of England.

Those of you who have grasped the concept of banks being able to create money out of nothing might be choking at the thought of them getting to keep the money that they've created when the borrower repays the loan. Fear not. In the same way that the bank creates money when it gives me a loan, the bank destroys money when I pay back the capital of the loan. If we consider my £1,200 loan that we discussed earlier, at the end of the first month I make a repayment of £58, which comprises £50 of capital and £8 of interest. The £50 capital repayment reduces my credit from the bank, and my debt to the bank, to £1,150. Money is credit-debt, so the amount of money that the bank created when it gave me the loan has been reduced by £50. The £50 that I've repaid is destroyed – it disappears into thin air from whence it came. This means that most of the money in the UK economy is temporary money – it exists for as long as it takes to repay the loan that caused it to be created. It's easy to see where the money comes from to repay the loan capital – it was created by the bank when I took out the loan, was spent by me into the economy and then returned to me via my earnings over the period of the loan. It's less easy to see where the money comes from to pay the interest of £8 a month. Unlike the loan capital (£1,200), which is destroyed as it's paid back, the interest is permanent money that the bank uses to pay overheads, salaries, bonuses, and dividends. A little of it (very little) might have been created by the Bank of England as notes but most of it will be money that the banks created when they made a loan to someone else. The money that I use to pay interest on my loan is money that was created by a bank for your loan. You spent the money that the bank lent to you into the general economy, it came to me as part of my earnings and I gave it to the bank as interest on my loan. The money that you use to pay interest on your loan is money that was created when your neighbour took out a loan and spent it into the general economy, and so on. Obviously, the only way that this can work is for the banks to be busy making lots of new loans all the time, creating new money every day to replace the money that they're gathering for themselves as interest. The important point to understand here is that the money the banks get paid as interest becomes permanent money. This is the alchemy of banking. Banks create money out of thin air and use some of it to pay their overheads and to make bankers rich. The process works as long as the banks have a supply of willing borrowers for whom they can create a supply of new money, some of which they can capture and turn into permanent money for themselves. It sounds extraordinary, but it's true.

Our culture loves money but disapproves of debt – having lots of money is good but being in debt is bad. This general disapproval of debt shows us that there's a general ignorance of what money actually is. As soon as we learn that almost all of the money in our economy is debt (even banknotes are debts owed by the Bank of England to the bearer of the note) we have to concede that our disapproval of debt is ridiculous. We are all participants in debt, all of the time. I cannot have £1,000 in the bank unless someone else is £1,000 in debt. If I am in debt to the tune of £1,000 it means that someone else has £1,000 of money that wouldn't otherwise exist. Perhaps our disapproval of debt is really a fear of not being able to repay what we owe. If the money that we have agreed to repay on a loan each month is persistently more than the money that we have available for repayments, then we have a problem. But the problem is exactly the same as not having enough money to pay the gas bill or buy groceries. A loan is just another purchase that requires regular payments, the same as gas or groceries. We might be justified in disapproving of an individual who is unable to repay a loan – he shouldn't have tried to 'live beyond his means' – but if we look at personal debt collectively, our disapproval doesn't make sense. The only reason that any of us have any money to pay for gas or groceries or loan repayments is because the money was lent to someone by a bank. If we all stopped borrowing money and paid off all of our loans there would be hardly any money left in the economy. Your employer wouldn't have any money to pay your salary. You wouldn't have any money to pay your bills. The government wouldn't have any money to give you as benefits. The economy would seize up. Disapproving of debt is stupid. Debt is money and money is what makes our society work.

Let's go back to our earlier question: how many of these 'units of account' that we call money are in the UK economy? The answer is a very big number, and big numbers can be confusing. Since the financial crisis of 2007/08 we have become used to hearing about billions and trillions of pounds, dollars and euros but many of us have only a hazy idea of just how big a billion or a trillion actually is, which isn't helped by the fact that, until recently, different definitions of billion and trillion were being used on opposite sides of the Atlantic. Thankfully everyone agrees on the definition of a million and most people know what its value is (a thousand thousands) and what it looks like when written down (1,000,000 - which is often abbreviated to £1M). So, in an attempt to reduce confusion, I'm going to use millions whenever I refer to a big number. Ten million pounds will be written as £10M, a thousand million pounds as £1,000M, and so on. Back to answering the question. The Bank of England keeps records of the UK's the money supply – statistics that give an approximation of the amount of money in the UK economy in any particular month. In March 2012 the total money supply was around £2,336,000M, of which £62,000M was coins and notes, £218,000M was central bank reserves, and £2,056,000M was digital money in commercial bank accounts. So the vast majority of the UK's money supply is created and held by the commercial banks. This digital money is created by banks when they make loans and is destroyed as the loans are repaid, so the total amount of this type of money in the economy is always changing.

We've now got a good idea of what money is, where it comes from, and how much of it we have sloshing about in the UK economy. Let's now have a look at what we do with money, and how we feel about it. Every breath that we take in life is made easier by money. Our lungs are powered by the food that we eat, and every morsel of food that we put in our mouths is the result of a vast and complex network of human activity that we call 'the economy'. Just think for a moment about what is involved in the production and delivery of slice of toast to the breakfast table. Think of all the ore that was mined and smelted and bashed and rolled to produce the metals to build every bit of machinery that was used to cultivate, harvest, process, and deliver the ingredients for the bread, and then bake the loaf and deliver it to the shop, and then transport it to your kitchen and then slice it and turn it from bread into toast. The number of commercial transactions that took place to put that slice of toast on your plate is mind-boggling. Trying to make all of these transactions work smoothly without the use of money would be extremely difficult. Exchange of goods and services is what makes our lives secure and enjoyable, and money makes exchange easy. Thanks to money we can get prompt payment for our labour and immediately transfer ownership of stuff from one person to another. The speed and reliability of these transactions are what allow our economy to thrive, making it easy for everyone to join in the business of exchange regardless of ability and timescales. Money allows me to buy what I need today even if I don't produce anything useful this month. I might be on holiday, or planning a new business venture, or I might be too old and frail to work. Whatever the reason for my idleness, using money as a means of exchange allows me to offset my time as a producer from my time as a consumer. Having money to exchange for stuff means that I can participate in the economy at any time, not just when I have produced something that other people might want.

Using money as a means of exchange is genius.

The other thing that we do with money is hoard it. When we get more money than we need for day-to-day living we end up with a surplus that we can hold onto for spending at a later date. This is using money as a store of value. As described above, a pile of spare money is useful for smoothing out spikes in our getting-and-spending patterns, and for funding occasional large purchases – a car or a holiday, for example. It's also useful as insurance against unforeseen circumstances. Having money – the happy state between getting and spending it – is one of the main drivers of our culture. Everyone wants to have more money. On the face of it this seems to be perfectly logical. Having money means that I can buy what I want when I want it, so if I have lots of money I can buy more of what I want whenever I want it. But our culture takes the desire for hoarding money away beyond this. The ownership of money has become an end in itself. No matter how much money someone owns, if they have an opportunity to capture more, they'll take it. This doesn't merely apply to the super-rich whose faces appear in celebrity magazines. Many of us have money that we will never spend in our lifetime. Having it appears to be more important that spending it: quantity appears to be more important than utility. This collective fetish for hoarding money is perverse because money only becomes valuable when we spend it. When money's sitting in our bank account or in a bag under the bed it's essentially useless – a line of numbers in a computer or a pile of paper. Our stored money is nothing more than a promise of future usefulness. In fact, a store of money comes with a burden of worry. What if someone burgles the house and steals the bag of notes? Or what if the house burns down? The promise of future spending power is gone. And what about money in the bank? In 2011 the real rate of inflation was considerably greater than the interest I was getting on my savings. My promised future spending power was shrinking every day. Stored money is nothing more than an unreliable promise of spending power sometime in an unforeseeable future. Money in the bank is nothing more substantial than hope. We anticipate that we will be able to use it to buy something that we want but it has no tangible value until the moment that it's spent. A lot of people will be struggling to get their heads around this idea that stored money is useless until it's spent, so let's think about two identical piles of banknotes - £10,000 in each pile – and you are allowed to choose one or the other. One of the piles of money is for hoarding and the other is for spending but you don't know which is which. If you choose the hoarding pile it gets locked in a safe and you're not allowed to touch it for 100 years. If you choose the spending pile you have to spend it all within a year and the only things that you're allowed to buy with it are consumables – food, drink, fuel, and the like. Whichever pile you choose you're going to be £10,000 wealthier on the day that you make your choice. If you choose the spending pile your new wealth will dwindle to nothing over 12 months. If you choose the hoarding pile you're going to be £10,000 richer for the rest of your life. Our culture suggests that we should hope to choose the hoarding pile – everyone wants to be permanently richer – but common sense tells us we should hope to choose the spending pile because the other pile, the £10,000 that's locked in the safe for 100 years, is obviously useless. If you're thinking that this is a silly scenario that bears no relation to real life, consider the thousands of people who die every year with £10,000 in their bank accounts – money that's just as useless as the £10,000 in the hypothetical safe. "But," I hear you say, "in the real world the deceased can pass on their store of money to their heirs." Yes they can, and the heirs might blow the £10,000 on a world cruise, but our culture would frown on that. We would be much more approving if the heirs kept the £10,000 in the bank and passed it on in their wills to the next generation, having carefully held onto it for years without spending a single penny. The first point to take from this is that money can only be considered as a store of value if the intention is to spend it at some point in the foreseeable future. If there is no intention to spend it then stored money is utterly useless, doing nothing more than giving us the illusion of being wealthy. The second point to understand is that the true value of money can only be measured at the moment that it's spent, and its value is determined by the price of whatever the money is being used to buy. Let's suppose it's February and I am thinking of buying a second-hand car. I decide that I want an X-type Jaguar that's around three years old and I have a budget of £12,000. I find dozens of X-types advertised for sale for around £9,000. Then I get distracted by other things so I keep driving my old car and the money stays in my bank account. In October I get around to thinking about buying my Jag but now they have become scarce and the few that are available are priced around £12,000. From the perspective of Jag-buying the money in my bank account has lost 25% of its value in just 8 months. The prices of the things that we want to buy are changing all the time so the potential value of the money that we have in store is changing all of the time, and the actual value of the money that we have in store can only be determined at the moment that we spend it. Money, therefore, is an unreliable store of value for future purchases and utterly useless if it is never used to purchase anything.

At this point I can hear some of you protest that money left in the bank indefinitely is a very good store of value because the bank pays you interest on it. Well, yes, you do get interest payments for the money that you leave in the bank but there's no guarantee that the amount you get paid in interest will be greater than the loss in value due to general inflation. For much of 2011/12 I was being paid 2.3% interest on the money in my account while real inflation was running at around 5%, so my money in the bank was losing value. The other thing to understand about interest payments is that they are your share of the profits that are generated by the bank's commercial activities. When you put money into your bank account you might feel as though you're depositing a store of value for yourself but you're actually investing in a profit-making business – the bank. Far from being a store of value your money becomes risk capital that the bank uses to back up the loans that it makes to householders and businesses. If, in the UK, you have less than £85,000 in your account the risk is relatively low because deposits up to this value are underwritten by the taxpayer but the fact remains that depositing money in the bank means that you are gambling on the competence and probity of the bankers and the people with whom they do business.

Despite my best efforts many of you will be unconvinced that money is an unreliable store of value. Having some spare money set aside gives us a very strong sense of security whereas having no spare money makes us feel very vulnerable. Money in the bank makes us feel safe. However, the unreliability of money as a store of wealth means that we are often disappointed by the value of our money when we remove it from the store and try to spend it. Inflation, general and specific, and the variable competence of bankers mean that long-term stores of wealth like pensions or endowment mortgages often end up providing much less money than they originally promised. Such examples are sober reminders of how the value of stored money can diminish over time. There is no doubt that everyone benefits from having a financial buffer – an amount of money that can be used to smooth out the bumps between getting and spending – but there is nothing to say that this has to take the form of money in the bank. And the notion that a personal store of hundreds of thousands of pounds is required for financial security is absolutely ridiculous. Holding onto more money than you'll ever need to use as a financial buffer makes no sense whatsoever. All stored money is stagnant, but money that's stored forever and never put to use is beyond stagnant: it's dead. Our cultural obsession with money as a store of value may be explained by our fear of poverty and our desire to feel wealthy, but these are poor excuses for misusing money in this way. Money as a means of exchange is genius, but every time we stuff a little bit more of it into the bank to increase our sense of security and wealth we make it a little bit harder for our economy to prosper.

3 | Economy

When I was a boy I read a children's adaptation of the story of Robinson Crusoe and wanted nothing more than to be washed up on a deserted island and left to live off my wits and whatever the island provided. The idea of building a house from sticks and leaves, hunting wild goats, catching fish, and eating berries seemed like the most exciting adventure that a boy could possibly be lucky enough to have. The reality of surviving as an individual on planet earth is, of course, much more brutal than my Robinson Crusoe storybook. Being left to fend for yourself is to be condemned to a life of extreme physical hardship. Everything that we need to do in order to survive and everything that we enjoy in the way of material comfort is much easier to get with the help of other people. Every morsel of food that you eat, every thread of clothing on your body, every bit of timber and steel and glass and concrete that makes up the house in which you live are there to keep you fed and clothed and sheltered only because of the collaboration of hundreds of thousands of individuals in the planning and doing of millions of tasks. This is 'the economy', a bubbling ferment of trades and exchanges that's fuelled by our individual needs and desires interacting in a system that is mind-boggling in its complexity and lubricated throughout by money. The getting and spending of money is what allows us to collaborate so easily with each other to provide ourselves with all of the things that we need and enjoy. Money is what makes our economy work.

The hustle and bustle of everyday life can make us blind to the necessity of some sections of our economy and over-emphasise the importance of others. The bit of our economy in which food is grown, harvested and distributed is absolutely essential to our personal survival – if we don't have any food to eat we will die – but few of us pay much attention to the economics of farming, fishing, or food distribution. We expect to be able to walk into a supermarket and fill the trolley with whatever takes our fancy. We are similarly blasé about necessities such as water and fuel. When water becomes scarce life becomes very difficult and when fuel is unavailable our winters will kill us, yet we tend to take these things for granted expecting them to be available at all times without any thought as to how they are delivered to us. This lack of appreciation for how life's necessities are provided contrasts sharply with our interest in the bits of the economy that give us the things that we desire. Our culture is obsessed with the economy of our aspirations – the houses in which we live, their location, their market value, and whether we own them or rent them. We judge ourselves by the clothes that we wear, the cars that we drive, the schools that our children attend, the mobile phones that we use, and the amounts of money that we receive as salaries. Our interest in economics doesn't extend far beyond our personal economy – our income, our mortgage, our pension, our household bills – and this means that our understanding of the wider economy is woefully weak. When grim economic news appears on our screens we blame the government or the bankers or the super-rich and we huff and puff and say something should be done, but we have no clear idea what should be done because we are largely ignorant of how the economy functions. We all sat through compulsory lessons in English and arithmetic at school but few of us were forced to study how the economy of our world works. This lack of economic education means that few of us have any idea of the shape of our economy or any understanding of how its component parts interact to provide us with all of the stuff that we take for granted and all of the stuff that we crave. Macroeconomics is the word that's used to describe the big economic picture and before we can hope to make our money work properly we have to get ourselves into a position where we can see the big picture and make sense of what we're looking at.

A good place to start when trying to understand macroeconomics is raw materials. Everything that we use to feed, house, transport, and entertain us is made up of a variety of stuff that we found or grew somewhere on the planet. The people who mine for ore, drill for oil, manage our forests, catch our fish, and cultivate the fields in which our food is grown form the foundations of our economy. On the next layer are the people who process the raw materials into stuff that can be used to make other stuff. Steelmakers, oil refiners, saw-millers, fish processers, grain millers, and the like. After them come the people who make things from the processed materials that can be used in the manufacture and assembly of finished products. We can call these people component makers and this is where our economy explodes into such quantity and variety of activity that the mind finds it impossible to comprehend. And then there are the people who assemble the finished products that we buy – bread rolls, fish fingers, oven-ready pizza, ball-point pens, televisions, toilet paper, windows, pillows, central heating boilers, electric light switches, dustbins, cars, shoes, telephones, sofas, refrigerators, shampoo, pepper grinders – the list is endless. Alongside these people who transform raw materials into finished products are people who help to make it all happen as smoothly as possible – lawyers who make the contracts, cleaners who keep the workplace safe and pleasant, accountants who manage the finances, cooks who feed the workforce, administrators who keep the records, drivers who move people and stuff to where they are needed, managers who organise the teams, IT technicians who keep the systems running, and so on. And then there are the teachers who educate, the medics who heal, the carers who look after the frail, the roadmen who fill the potholes, the dustmen who deal with the rubbish, the linesmen who keep the electricity on, the engineers who keep the fresh water flowing in and the foul water flowing out, the storytellers who make the movies, the journalists who write the news, the singers who sing, the comedians who make us laugh, the politicians who make policy, the civil servants who make it happen, the social workers who help the damaged and the feckless, the bankers who manage our money, the police officers who catch the criminals, the midwives who deliver our babies, the undertakers who take care of the dead, and all of the other thousands of people who do all the things that are done so that we can live the lives that we live. This is our economy. It runs wide and deep through our society, extending across national borders, reaching up into the highest echelons of wealth and power and down into the poorest communities on the planet. The economy connects everyone to everyone else in a thousand different ways and affects how we live from the moment that we're born until the day we die. Life is economics and the better we understand how the economy works the more chance we have of making life easier to live.

The economy is frighteningly complex but the one thing that connects every part of it to every other part is money. Almost everything that happens in our economic life involves the transfer of money from one person to another. Understanding how money moves through our economy seems like a good way of understanding how our economy works. There appear to be three sectors of the economy in which getting and spending money work in distinctly different ways – commerce, banking, and government.

Commerce is often called 'the private sector', where people and businesses buy and sell goods and services from each other. In general the activity of this sector can be described as productive and useful. We might argue about the relative usefulness of growing potatoes and selling nail polish but there is demand for both potatoes and nail polish so both can be described as productive. When I buy a bag of potatoes I give the shopkeeper money, some of which he spends on buying the potatoes from the wholesaler and paying for the overheads of the shop, and the rest he keeps for himself. This is the bit that we call profit. The commercial sector is driven by the desire for profit. Even the most socialist-minded wholefood co-operative has to turn a profit in order to continue in business, and most people who participate in the commercial sector are keen to capture as much profit as they possibly can for themselves. Most commercial enterprises need to buy some stuff before they can start trading – equipment, stock, premises, etc. The money that's used to pay for these set-up costs is called capital and the aim of the suppliers of capital is to get back more money than they put into the business. So the first bit of profit that a new business generates pays back the original capital, and from then on the profits are added to the wealth of the investors – if the business is successful the investors get rich. The commercial sector is competitive. Every entrepreneur wants their business to be better and more profitable than the one next door, which means that they are all aiming to capture as much money as they possibly can. Successful entrepreneurs hold onto a proportion of the money that their business captures every month, removing it from the pool of money that flows through the economy. Over time, a significant amount of money gets captured and hoarded by successful business owners. We think of people who have a lot of money as being big spenders and they're certainly inclined to splash out on big houses, expensive cars, private yachts, and the like. But the effect of this spending doesn't filter very far through the commercial economy. One person spending £1M on a yacht will never be as distributive as a thousand people spending £1,000 each on general living expenses. The other tendency of rich people is to have very large bank balances. If you think that this means the banks will be lending the rich people's money into the commercial economy, replacing the money that the rich people have captured, you'd be mistaken. The amount of money that a bank holds on deposit can influence the amount of money that it creates in the form of loans but there is no direct relationship between the two. The successful entrepreneur can deposit £1M in the bank but there's no guarantee that this will prompt the bank to make £1M of new loans to the productive economy. Our economy runs on money. If money is available and mobile our economy thrives: people are able to buy lots of things from lots of different businesses. If money is scarce people are limited to buying fewer things from a smaller range of businesses. So when successful entrepreneurs capture and hoard significant amounts of money they cause the amount of economic activity in the commercial sector to decrease. And here we have the paradox of the commercial economy – it can thrive only if money is available and mobile, but commercial success tends to reduce the availability and mobility of money. The negative effects of this paradox are compounded by the fact that the richer an individual becomes the easier it is for her to capture even more money, leaving even less of it available for commercial activity. In the commercial sector money inevitably flows uphill into the hands of relatively few individuals where much of it gets stuck. Left to its own devices, the commercial economy will always end up starving itself of the money that it needs in order to function. Thank goodness for banks.

The banking sector likes to pretend that it's just another bit of the commercial economy, but it isn't. As we discovered earlier, banks are unique because they're able to create the money that pays for their overheads and profits. They're also unique because they control, to a large extent, how much money is in the economy and where that money is originally spent. Money that's created by banks as loans is what feeds the commercial sector, replacing the money that the successful entrepreneurs have taken out of general circulation. When people and businesses find themselves short of money (because other people are hoarding lots of it) they borrow from the banks. The vitality of our economy is therefore determined by the willingness of banks to lend. Generally, banks are very willing to lend money because that's what makes bankers rich. Let's have another look at what happens when the bank lends me £1,200. When giving me the loan the bank creates money, a credit-debt relationship between me and the bank in which the bank owes me £1,200. When I spend the money the credit-debt relationship is transferred to new parties (the seller of the thing that I buy and their bank) so this money has gone into the economy and no-one can tell that it was created out of thin air by my bank. My bank and I have conspired to add £1,200 to the general economy. But the other side of the credit-debt relationship between me and the bank still exists. I still owe my bank £1,200. You could say that when the bank lent me £1,200 it actually created £2,400 of new money, half of which it gave to me to spend, while the other half was added to the bank's balance sheet as an asset. The bank can't go and spend this money on beer and pizza but it does make the bank look a little bit bigger than it was before it gave me the loan. The bigger a bank appears to be, the more able it is to borrow money from other banks which it can use in all sorts of cunning ways to capture even more money for itself. So when a bank lends money it not only gets an income from the interest that it charges on the loan, it also creates more opportunities to do more business and generate bigger profits.

We've already seen how the money that I use to make interest payments on my loan must come from a bank creating money by making a loan to someone else. Our economy will run out of money unless the banks keep lending, but a bank's willingness to lend is restricted by two very powerful forces. The first of these is confidence. If the bank isn't confident that borrowers will be able to repay loans, it will not lend. The less banks lend, the less money is available for people with existing loans to pay the interest on them, but the interest must still be paid. Every interest payment that's made removes money from the commercial economy. If the banks aren't recycling this money back into the economy by spending it or making new loans, people find money hard to come by. When money is scarce people are less able (or less inclined) to spend, and when people aren't spending businesses are less inclined to invest. So the banks' reluctance to lend creates a climate in which businesses are reluctant to spend their hoards of spare money or borrow new money from the banks. Meanwhile everyone is paying off their loans, including the interest, which means there's even less money available for commercial activity. This is a classic case of negative feedback – the worse the problem gets, the worse it gets. The other powerful force that restricts a bank's willingness to lend is the desire of the directors and shareholders of the bank to be richer tomorrow than they are today. Instead of lending money for productive activities in the commercial sector, banks can capture more money with less risk by lending to speculators who are gambling on the prices of all sorts of things which they like to call assets. Even better, the banks can create a climate in which certain asset prices will rise and then encourage speculators to join the fun. The housing market bubble is a classic example of this. By making it easy for people to borrow money against property the banks caused house prices to rise, which made everyone think that they could 'make money' from buying and selling property. Lots of people borrowed money to buy property, so the property prices rose even further. Every mortgage that the banks approved meant a significant long term income stream in the form of interest payments. If you take out an interest-only mortgage of £100,000 at 5% p.a. and repay it over a period of 20 years, the bank will end up with £100,000 of interest payments. The bank captures £5,000 a year for 20 years for very little effort and even less risk. Compare that with investing £100,000 in a small business where someone in the bank has to make a judgement about the business's viability, and then arrange some sort of security over the assets of the business owner, and then monitor the progress of the business over the period of the loan, which is probably only 7 years and will earn the bank less than £19,000 of interest, a paltry £2,700 a year in return for all that hard work and additional risk. For the banker with ambitions of pocketing a multi-million pound bonus it's an easy choice – mortgage lending is the way to go. So, although banks do provide additions to the money supply of the general economy, these additions are temporary and are targeted at sectors that the bankers think are most profitable, which are not necessarily areas of the economy that you and I would call productive. Where the banking sector can claim to be the same as the commercial sector is in its net effect on the availability and mobility of money. Banks and bankers, like businesses and business owners, are inveterate hoarders of money. Where the banking sector differs is its ability to control the amount of money that's created to fuel the commercial economy and where that money is originally spent. People who are fortunate enough to live and work in parts of the commercial economy that are favoured by the banks find that money is available and mobile, which makes life easy. People who are outside the favoured areas of the economy have the opposite experience: money is scarce, and fear of ending up with none means people who have it are inclined to hold onto it. Banks have no remit to distribute money throughout the economy so that everyone gets their fair share. Banks are businesses whose primary aim is to capture as much money as possible on behalf of their shareholders. In an economy where banks control the money supply there will always be poverty amongst the people who are not favoured by the banks' patronage. Prompted partly by compassion and partly by fear of civil unrest, our modern response to the poverty that arises out of commerce and banking is to divert some of the money that is flowing towards the top of the pile and use it to provide useful services to the population as a whole and basic support for people who have been bypassed by the banks' largesse. This is known as 'the public sector' which is run by various layers of government.

The government collects money from the economy by insisting that we pay taxes. Even the poorest of the poor pay some sorts of tax and from there on up the pyramid of wealth, everyone is liable for a range of taxes that are levied on practically everything you can think of – earnings, retail sales, housing, vehicles, fuel, employment, capital gains, and many more. Tax money pours into the Treasury and is distributed via a bewildering catalogue of government agencies to fund a wide array of services – education, health, transport, housing, environmental protection, defence, and so on – most of which are free at point of use to the citizens of the UK. Another chunk of the tax take is given to people who are unable to get enough money from elsewhere to meet their monthly needs – the elderly, the infirm, and people who are unable or unwilling to find paid employment. The remainder of the tax money is used to pay for the administration and delivery of these public services, including the costs of parliament and the government of the day. The problem with taxes is that we hate to pay them and will avoid doing so if we possibly can. At the same time we make continuous demands for improvements to the range and quality of services that the government provides, which almost always cost more money. The result of this collective schizophrenia is that we never give government enough money to do all the things that we demand it does for us. It's generally considered a bad idea to allow governments to print money to fund the services that it provides – experience suggests that politicians in search of votes will print too much money, which reduces the value of it, which ends up doing more harm than good to the economy (and the reputation of the politician). Instead of printing money the government sells bonds and uses the money that it gets from the sale of the bonds to cover the costs of government that we're not prepared to pay for via taxes. A government bond is nothing more complicated than a record of a loan from the buyer of the bond to the government. It's a fixed term loan with an agreed interest payment. Government bonds are typically bought by pension funds, banks, other financial institutions, and successful money hoarders, all of whom are quite happy to lend to government because such loans are considered low risk – governments have guaranteed income from taxes and they (almost) never go bust. Some of the money that the government pays as interest on the bonds filters back into the general economy via pension payments and dividends to people with modest investment incomes but a significant chunk of it gets captured by people who already have large hoards of money that they use for financial gambling or simply sit on because it makes them feel rich.. The effect of government borrowing is the same as the effect of commercial borrowing – both suck money out of the commercial economy into the hands of a relatively small number of individuals and institutions, where it tends to get stuck.

Between the government and the commercial banking sector we have the central bank – the Bank of England – which is supposed to be independent from both the commercial sector and government. In reality the Bank of England has very close ties to both big business and the government of the day. The most obvious contribution of the Bank of England to the money in our economy is bank notes, which it has the power to print or destroy as it sees fit. This has a small effect on the total amount of money in the economy. The Bank of England also tries to protect our economy from becoming unstable in a couple of ways. It attempts to control the mobility of money by varying the base (or minimum) interest rate. In theory, raising the interest rate will discourage spending (and slow down the rate of inflation), while lowering the interest rate will encourage spending and boost the economy (and increase the rate of inflation). However, the period between 2009 and 2012 when the interest rate was lowered from (an already low) 2% to 0.5% and held there, suggest that the theory is nonsense. During these three years the UK economy stayed stubbornly stagnant. The second way that the Bank of England tries to keep the economy stable is by controlling the amount of money that the commercial banks have to hold in reserve as insurance against some of their loans going bad or a large number of depositors wanting their money back all at the same time. By insisting that commercial banks hold more in reserve the Bank of England can, in theory, reduce the amount of money in the economy. In reality commercial banks decide how much to lend based on their confidence that the borrower will be able to repay the loan. The bank official who issues the loan does not check to see what the bank's loan:reserve ratio is. He makes the loan first and the reserves to back it up are found afterwards. At the end of each day the banks reconcile what they owe to each other and then check to see if they have enough reserves at the Bank of England to balance their books. If they find they're short of reserves they can borrow what they need from another bank, or they can borrow from the Bank of England itself. The reserve requirements set by the Bank of England therefore do little or nothing to control the amount of money that's created by commercial banks in the form of loans. In recent years, in response to persistent recession, the Bank of England has employed a different tactic to try to get the economy moving again. It has created billions of pounds of new money which it has spent on buying government bonds from banks, pension funds and the like in the hopes that these institutions would use the cash to invest in the commercial economy. This process is euphemistically called "quantitative easing" which sounds very technical but it's really just creating digital money out of thin air and giving it to the banks. Unfortunately the banks appear to have used this money to bolster their reserves and speculate on asset prices rather than invest it in the productive economy. The truth about the Bank of England is that it has very little power to influence the amount of money in the economy or how the money is used.

The economy of the UK, like every nation in the world, extends beyond its own borders. We buy stuff from people in other countries, things that are unavailable or more expensive in our own, and we sell our own products and services to customers abroad. This international trade relies on foreign exchange. If my company sells whisky to someone in Japan my customer has to exchange yen for pounds sterling before they can pay me for the whisky. If my company buys machinery from Germany it has to exchange pounds for euros in order to make the purchase. The number of pounds that the Japanese client gets for their yen, or the number of euros that my company gets for its pounds, is rarely constant because the exchange rates between currencies are always on the move, pushed up and down in relation to each other by a variety of forces. Currency traders can move exchange rates by selling lots of one currency and buying lots of another. The performance of an individual economy in relation to its trading partners can also affect the exchange rate of its national currency. A government can manipulate the exchange rate of its currency by encouraging its central bank to ease or tighten monetary policy, and by controlling the import and export of goods and services. Varying exchange rates can have a significant effect on a nation's international competitiveness. A strong (high value) currency makes exports expensive and imports cheap, while a weak (low value) currency makes imports expensive and exports cheap. If a currency is too strong the nation's businesses struggle to export their products and the nation's consumers favour less expensive imports from other countries. When this occurs native businesses lose customers at home and abroad, which means that their production falls, which leads to fewer jobs and reduced tax revenues. If a currency is too weak the price of imports rises and if these imports are essential for the economy to operate (e.g. oil) then the economy suffers. It's in everyone's interest to keep exchange rates at a level where they don't disadvantage the national economy either way. Using a currency as a store of value can have significant effects on its price on the foreign exchange markets. A currency's exchange rate depends to a large extent on how much appetite there is for holding it as a store of value. If the currency is seen as a safe haven lots of people want to buy it so the price goes up relative to other currencies. If investors think the country is in economic trouble, or has political leaders that appear untrustworthy, or the government is actively devaluing the currency, its usefulness as a store of value will diminish, people who have it will sell it, so the price will drop. These changes in the value of a currency relative to other currencies that are commonly used for international trade (primarily the US dollar but also the euro, yen, Swiss franc, and pound sterling) can have a significant effect on the health of a national economy. The manipulation of currency values by governments and foreign exchange traders can trigger economic problems that are extremely serious for national and international economies, more of which later.

We now have an overall picture of where money comes from and how it moves through our economy. Most of it is created by banks as loans to the commercial sector where it bounces around, facilitating exchange between individuals and businesses. Some of this money flows out of the commercial sector into government coffers and then back to the commercial sector via government spending. All the while a steady trickle of this money flows into the hands of a relatively small number of wealthy individuals and companies where some of it is used to fund whatever activities are most likely to add more money to their hoards and some is just left sitting doing nothing except making its owners feel rich. Whether by design or accident, this is how our economy works. There are conspiracy theorists who will tell you that the system has been designed and manipulated by a rich and powerful elite whose members delight in controlling every aspect of our lives for their own gain. Others suggest that the rich and powerful are merely opportunists who have taken advantage of a system that has evolved from a messy history of human interactions where our ignorance and stupidity have given licence to the avarice of the rich. To counter these disparaging views of our economic system there's a strong body of opinion that sees it as the means by which we have progressed from brutal lives of marginal survival to the astonishing material comfort and security that many of us now enjoy. Whichever side of the argument you are inclined to take there is plenty of evidence that our system is far from perfect. At the time of writing this book many of the world's economies are in recession and an economic catastrophe looms in Europe. Behind the headlines of currency crises and banking bail-outs there are millions of stories of human hardship and tragedy. The evidence is all around us – our economic system is dysfunctional – but the tangle of competing diagnoses of multiple malfunctions makes it very hard to come to any clear understanding of what's causing the turmoil, and without an understanding of the causes it's impossible to decide what should be done to sort it all out.

4 | Dysfunction

The complexity of our economic system makes it hard for us to see where its flaws are even when the effects of its dysfunction are so glaringly obvious. Sometimes a complex problem is easier to understand through analogy, so let's consider this little tale and see what we can learn from it.

A small island lying off the coast of the UK has been having a tough time during the recession. The tourist industry, normally the mainstay of the island's economy, has been very slow for the last few years and this has had a cumulative effect. If anyone has any spare money, they're not keen to spend it, so all of the island's businesses are suffering. A visitor arrives off the morning ferry and makes his way to the hotel where he pays for his room in advance with a £50 note. The hotelier has nothing to feed the visitor for breakfast so she takes the £50 note down to the village shop. Having £50 that she wasn't expecting encourages her to splash out on goodies for her family as well as breakfast ingredients for the visitor. The shopkeeper is delighted with £50 of sales that he hadn't anticipated and decides to use the windfall to pay off his debt to the local farmer who supplies the shop with eggs. The farmer is very happy with the £50 note because he can fill up his truck with fuel, which he does at the garage. The owner of the garage now has the visitor's £50 note which he takes down to the hotel to pay off his bar tab, to the delight of the hotelier. Meanwhile the visitor has had a phone call to say that his poor old mother has broken her leg and he has to go home on the afternoon ferry. He asks the hotelier to refund the money that he paid in advance for the room, which she does by giving him back the £50 note. The visitor goes home, a few hours after he arrived, taking the £50 note with him. Nobody on the island has any more money than they had before the visitor arrived but the hotelier has bacon and eggs in the fridge as well as some treats for her family. The shopkeeper has cleared his £50 debt to the farmer, who has a full tank of fuel in his truck, and the garage owner has paid off his tab at the bar. For a short while the economy of the island was working again, all thanks to the temporary presence of a £50 note.

For the productive economy to work all that's required is for money to be available and mobile.

Let's change the plot a little and see what happens. The farmer is a bit of a miser. He pretends that he's as hard up as everyone else on the island but he's got plenty money in the bank. He grows most of his own food, has his own woodland for firewood, and buys diesel in bulk from a mainland supplier, so he doesn't need to spend much of his money into the economy of the island. When the shopkeeper gives him the £50 note to pay off the egg debt, the farmer puts the money into his bank account. Now the garage owner doesn't have any spare money to pay off his bar tab and the hotelier doesn't have the £50 note to return to the visitor. By using the £50 note as a store of value, instead of spending it, the farmer has left both the garage owner and the hotelier in debt.

When money is hoarded it ceases to be of use to the productive economy.

In this version of the story the hotelier is in a sticky situation. She has to give the visitor back his £50, but she's already spent it so what can she do? Luckily she's still got some slack in her overdraft, so she goes to the bank and withdraws £50 to give to the visitor. While she's in the bank the manager calls her through for a chat. He tells her that her application for a loan to buy a pizza oven has been rejected and that her overdraft limit will have to be reduced in line with the new policy of the bank. However, he has been authorised to offer her a mortgage on the hotel. She can use the mortgage money to clear the overdraft, buy the pizza oven, and have enough left over to redecorate the hotel and pay for an advertising campaign. Caught between a rock and a hard place the hotelier takes the plunge and agrees to the mortgage. By issuing the mortgage the bank creates new money in the hotelier's account, some of which she spends locally employing painters to decorate the rooms, an electrician to install the pizza oven, and a graphic designer to revamp the hotel's website. These people spend some of the money that they've earned into the local economy, which means more businesses on the island have more money passing through their hands, which makes them feel more prosperous, and more inclined to spend.

The hotel's advertising campaign starts to bear fruit, bringing a trickle of visitors to the island. When they try the pizza they love it and tell all their friends on the mainland. Within a few months the hotel is busy with visitors who have heard about the amazing pizza. These visitors bring lots of money into the island, buying stuff from the shops as well as food and accommodation from the hotel. Within a year the economy of the island is booming and everyone has plenty of money to spend. In fact they all have more money than they need and the surplus piles up in their accounts at the bank. The money that the bank created and lent to the hotelier has given the economy of the island the kick-start that it needed. Money is widely available and moving freely around the island's economy, and between the island and the mainland. The increase in visitor numbers means that there's high demand for holiday accommodation. The bank sees an opportunity to do a lot of business on the island and starts to offer loans at very favourable rates. Lots of enterprising islanders decide to build new chalets and refurbish old cottages using the money that they've saved to lever large loans from the bank, which is very willing to lend. The shopkeeper takes a loan to build a new mini-supermarket and a local fisherman takes a loan to build a marina for visiting yachts. Now nobody has much money left in their savings accounts and they have large loan repayments to make every month, but the economy is booming so everyone is getting plenty of money flowing through their hands. The bank has a nice fat income stream from the interest on the loans and the entrepreneurs are doing good business letting holiday cottages and selling stuff to visitors.

Banks can make the productive economy thrive by providing money as debt.

In a few years fashions change and people go elsewhere for their holidays. The flood of visitors' money into the island slows to a trickle. By this time no-one is investing in any new ventures on the island so the bank has stopped creating new money in the form of loans. At first this isn't a problem because there's enough money circulating in the local economy to keep people spending, which keeps most of the local businesses afloat. But every month the island's entrepreneurs have to make hefty loan repayments to the bank. This steadily drains money out of the economy leaving less and less available for everyday commerce. Unless money comes from somewhere else to replace what the bank is extracting the island will certainly be bled dry. There are only two sources of money to replace what the bank is draining off every month. People can bring money to the island and spend it on pizza or property – there's currently a surplus of both on offer – or the bank can create new money in the form of loans. Holidaymakers are all going to the Mediterranean these days and the national property market has gone bust, so there's very little hope of anyone spending money into the island. Most of the property owners on the island are already mortgaged up to the hilt so the bank won't lend them any more money. The few people who are in a position to borrow money lack the confidence to invest in an island that's in recession. The islanders have nowhere to go to get new money and without money being available and mobile the economy of the island is stuffed.

Some people will blame the island's entrepreneurs for investing too heavily in holiday accommodation, but the result would have been exactly the same if they'd made more modest investments across a wider range of ventures. The problem isn't the choice of investment, the problem is that money is no longer available and mobile in the island economy, and the blame lies squarely with a system in which the availability of money to keep our economy running sweetly depends on the willingness of banks to lend and the appetite of people to borrow. If either one of these is reluctant to participate money becomes scarce and our economy stagnates. When bank lending is the main source of money in an economy a cycle of boom and bust is inevitable. In our island story, when the bank made loans to the entrepreneurs there was a massive spike in the island's money supply – lots of money was available and it was very mobile as the entrepreneurs spent it on building, equipping, and marketing their new businesses. The money that the bank created fuelled a boom on the island but as soon as the first loan repayments were made the slide from boom to bust commenced. The repayment money that represented the principal of the loans was destroyed as soon as it was repaid, steadily reducing the availability of money on the island. The repayment money that represented the interest on the loans was captured by the bank, and all but a tiny proportion of it (e.g. salaries of the local employees) left the island – a further steady reduction in the availability of money for everyday commerce on the island. When banks create money as loans they fuel economic exuberance by making money available and mobile. When the loans are repaid the banks destroy all of the money that they created *and* they suck significant amounts of additional money out of the economy in the form of interest. If the hotelier borrows £50,000 from the bank over 20 years at an interest rate of 5% per annum, by the time she's paid the mortgage off she will have given the bank c.£29,000 of interest in addition to repaying the £50,000 of capital. The temporary £50,000 boost to the island's money supply is followed by a long, slow seepage of £79,000 out of the island's economy. The destruction and sequestration of money by banks as loans are repaid will always leave an economy with less money available for everyday commerce unless new money is added to replace that which has been destroyed and sequestered.

Bank lending will always drain more money out of an economy than it puts in.

There are three ways that we can add money to the general economy to get us out of economic stagnation. Firstly, the people who have captured all the money – the bankers and their chums – can decide to spend it into the general economy. Some politicians and commentators seem to believe in this so-called 'trickle down' effect but it doesn't make any sense if you give it even a little bit of thought. There is a finite amount of money in the system and it cannot simultaneously be used as a store of wealth and a means of exchange. As long as we all want to increase our bank balances there will be a shortage of money flowing through the productive economy. Our second option is to tax the rich and redistribute the money into the economy via government programmes. This is wildly unpopular among the rich and they're generally very successful in their resistance to paying enough taxes to break the economy out of the spiral of decline. The third option, the one that we end up with by default, is to wait until enough people have paid off enough loans and are able and willing to take out new loans. When the banks start lending again, people have money to spend and the economy comes to life. Everyone breathes a sigh of relief, but as confidence returns and the bankers crank up the loan-making machinery the whole dysfunctional process starts all over again. At the heart of the problem is the influence that bankers have on the flow of money through the economy. The £50 note in our island story shows how the circulation of money makes an economy work. If money is available and mobile – able to flow continuously around an economy, driven organically by millions of interacting individual needs and desires – the economy will thrive. In our dysfunctional system the flow is linear, backwards and forwards between the banks and the economy, and is driven by the desire of bankers (and their shareholders) to capture more money today than they had yesterday. Bankers pump money into the economy when they see opportunities to capture a profit, then drain money back out of the economy in order to collect the profit. As a result we go from periods when we're swamped with money to periods when we're starved of it.

So we've identified the first major flaw in our system – the influence that bankers have on the way that money flows around our economy. The interest that the banks collect from borrowers obviously has a significant part to play in this. The money that banks collect as interest is what they use to cover their costs and pay the salaries, bonuses and dividends that make them and their shareholders rich. Bankers aren't the only people who profit from interest on loans. Everyone who has money in a savings account is doing it too. What we think of as our savings is actually a record of what we've lent to the bank in exchange for interest payments. These interest payments, minus bank charges and taxes, are the profits that we get from lending our money to the bank. Everyone is so used to this idea of using money to generate profits that we don't realise how damaging it is to the health of our economy. Let's go back to the island and see what happens when we get rid of the concept of interest being paid on borrowed money and replace it with the idea of getting a share of the profits of a venture in which we have invested.

Instead of the hotelier having a chat with the bank manager let's suppose that she fell into conversation with the farmer and told him of her ideas for sprucing up the hotel and installing a pizza oven. The farmer, miserly though he is, has a good eye for business and tells the hotelier he will back her venture. He'll give her the money that she needs to get the project underway and she'll pay him 10% of the gross profit in return. Now imagine that all of the other entrepreneurs on the island get the finance for their projects in a similar way – using money that somebody else has lying idle and wants to invest in holiday accommodation, or a mini-supermarket, or a marina, taking a percentage of the profits in return. When business is booming everyone's getting rich, much the same as when the bank lent the money. But what happens when the visitors stop coming and the money flowing into the island is reduced to a trickle? The gross profit earned by the hotelier will tumble to a tiny amount of money, but she'll only have to pay the farmer 10% of the tiny amount. This means that the cost of financing her venture goes up and down in concert with its profitability. In the good times everyone gets rich and in the bad times everyone tightens their belts. Contrast this scenario with the previous one where the hotelier borrowed from the bank and was forced to repay the same amount to the bank every month regardless of the profitability of the enterprise. Having the farmer invest in the project instead of borrowing from the bank is clearly much more sustainable from the perspective of the hotelier, and much more beneficial to the economy of the island because more of the money in the economy remains available for commercial activity.

When bankers lend money they like to think that they're investing in the business venture, or the house, or whatever the borrower intends to spend the money on, but they're mistaken. In the case of the hotelier the bank isn't investing in the pizza oven. All the bank is doing is giving money to the hotelier in return for a promise that she will repay it with interest. The correct term for this is usury. The farmer, on the other hand, has clearly made an investment in the hotelier's business. The return that he gets from his investment is directly proportional to the commercial success of the venture. This distinction between usury and investment is important. Usury is about renting out money in order to capture more money and places the bulk of risk squarely on the shoulders of the borrower. Investment is about sharing the profits of an enterprise where the burden of risk is shared by the investors in proportion to their input. More simply, usury is about 'making' money out of money whereas investment is about sharing the risks and rewards of enterprise. Usury is not the only way of 'making' money out of money. Bankers have invented many other methods of extracting profits by renting, exchanging, and otherwise speculating with money. Most of these activities are easy to participate in – all you need is a computer and someone who's good with numbers. This contrasts sharply with investments in the productive economy which tend to be less profitable and require expensive supervision by people who are skilled in assessing business prospects and are wise to the ways of the world. The problem with all of these activities where profits are made purely from manipulating money is that they ultimately reduce the availability of money (as in the case of usury), or the money that they manipulate never gets into the commercial economy at all (as in the case of currency speculation). This is a problem because the commercial economy is where the activities take place that provide us with the things that we need to sustain and enhance life. Manipulating money does nothing except transfer more money into the hands of the successful manipulators. We cannot eat money or use it to keep us warm and dry. Money won't transport us, nor will it entertain us. The commercial economy does all of these things but in order for it to work properly there has to be plenty of money available and circulating. Our dysfunctional economic system ensures that this happens for a limited amount of time before the money becomes scarce and the commercial economy seizes up, at which point we look to government for help. But government has its own problems to contend with.

In recent years it's become very fashionable to disapprove of government debt and demand that government borrowing is reduced. One way to achieve such a reduction in government debt is to maintain taxes at their current levels and reduce government spending, using the balance of the tax revenue to pay off the debt. The problem with this approach is that the money that would have been spent into the economy by the government is now being given to the banks where it's either destroyed (if it was created out of thin air when the bank bought the government bonds), or hoarded, or it gets used for speculation. This reduces the availability of money in the general economy, which reduces the opportunities for economic activity, which means that the government gets less tax revenue, which limits the ability of the government to reduce its debts. Another option for reducing government debt is to maintain government spending but increase taxes. Apart from being unpopular, this has the same effect as the previous option in that the extra tax money is diverted from the general economy to the banks, which reduces the opportunities for economic activity, which means the government gets less tax revenue, and so on. Whichever way we try to reduce government debt we end up with the same problem – a reduction in the amount of money available for general economic activity. The only way to reduce government debt and maintain a thriving economy is to replace the money that's being destroyed or hoarded (as government debt is paid off) with new money that's made available to the general economy. In our current system the only accepted way of adding new money to the productive economy is via bank lending – allowing the banks to create money when they make loans. So in order to get the money that we need to keep the economy thriving while we pay off government debt, we (individuals and businesses) have to borrow even more money from the banks. Some of you might argue that the government shouldn't have been so profligate to get into debt in the first place, but you're missing the point. The problem is that our economy runs almost entirely on money that's been created by the banks in the form of loans. It doesn't matter who takes out the original loan – government, businesses, individuals – what matters is that the loans must be repaid, and when we repay the loan both the principal and most of the interest are removed from the economy – they're no longer available for spending – and the only way to replace this money that we need to keep our economy thriving is to borrow it from a bank. Because of the way our system works we have a choice between economic stagnation or debt. It's always going to be one or the other. This dysfunction is built into our economic system but we make things even worse by our choice of targets for taxation.

A productive economy runs on confidence. When people who have money are confident that they can 'make money' from productive activities they'll be tempted to stop hoarding and start investing. When people who have the skills and enthusiasm to do productive things are confident that they'll be rewarded for working hard, they'll work hard and be productive. When people are confident that their jobs are secure and that the government is in good shape to look after them, they'll spend money on the things that the productive economy is producing. All of these things – investment, hard work, spending – are good for the economy and should be encouraged, but we actively discourage all of them by making them prime targets of our taxation system. National Insurance Contributions (NICs) are a direct tax on jobs. Employer's NICs add to the cost of providing a job and discourage employers from taking people on. Employee's NICs are paid by almost every employee, representing a significant tax on the income of every working person, especially those on low wages. Investment in productive activity is discouraged by both income and corporation taxes, which take away some of the money that's been captured through hard work and ingenuity. VAT is a direct tax on spending, adding a significant amount to the price of practically everything we buy. During the boom part of the cycle our taxation system is merely a discouragement to productive activity and spending but when we get to the bust end of it we see just how stupid we are to be taxing these things. When the economy is stagnant people lose their jobs and are unable to buy food or pay the rent. The stress of unemployment makes some of them ill. Lack of money drives others into crime. The government has to spend more on unemployment benefit, sickness benefit, healthcare, and the criminal justice system. Meanwhile tax revenues plummet. More than 90% of tax revenue comes from a combination of NICs, VAT, income and corporation taxes, all of which are reduced in times of economic stagnation. To try to pay for the increased costs of unemployment other areas of government spending get squeezed, spreading the pain wider and deeper into the economy. Inevitably government borrowing increases, which means the government has to pay more interest, which places further pressure on the Treasury's cashflow. When the economy slides into recession the government is stuck firmly between the devil and the deep blue sea. As tax revenues tumble downwards the cost of benefits soar upwards. Trying to fund benefits by taxing economic activity isn't the cleverest thing to do at the best of times, but when the going gets tough it's spectacularly stupid, guaranteeing a shortage of money for benefits when people are most in need.

In the midst of a recession one of the few things that a government can do to help revive the national economy is to devalue its own currency. The aim of this is to make the country's exports less expensive in foreign markets. There are several ways of devaluing a currency but the current favourite is buying government bonds with new money as we discussed earlier – so-called quantitative easing. One of the intentions of quantitative easing is to flood the foreign exchange markets with the national currency, thereby reducing its value which makes it easier for businesses to export their products, which the government hopes will stimulate the domestic economy. However, devaluing the currency also reduces the value of ordinary people's savings and causes inflation: prices go up because the value of the currency has gone down. The other side-effect can be a reactive devaluation of other currencies by their respective governments. When multiple countries devalue currencies at the same time they compete for the lowest value – a race to the bottom – which can cause hyperinflation and currency collapse. In the past efforts were made to prevent these currency wars by tying currencies into the market value of gold using international agreements such as the Gold Standard. This worked as long as the economies of all of the participating countries managed to maintain sustainable trade balances so that the value of their imports and exports were more or less the same. But when a country found itself struggling to export as much as it was importing it would break its currency's tie with gold and devalue. The Gold Standard was a nice idea but it never really worked when push came to shove, so it was abandoned. Variations in foreign exchange rates can be very disruptive to international trade and damaging to relationships between countries. Currency wars can easily turn into physical wars as nations try to protect their economies from depression and collapse. All of these problems arise from activity on the foreign exchange markets. Foreign exchange traders don't care about the social economies of nations whose currencies they trade. All they are interested in is betting the right way on the relative values of two or more currencies in order to capture as much profit as possible. Volatile foreign exchange markets are opportunities to get rich (if you make the right bet) but they're extremely damaging to productive economies that rely on stable currencies to provide predictable values for goods and services. Gambling with (or manipulating) currency values is probably the most destructive thing that we can do with our money. The fact that we allow such gambling to take place is yet another indication of how dysfunctional our economic system is. The productive economy on which we all depend for our material comfort is continually enfeebled by the manipulation of our money by bankers and traders whose primary motivation is to make themselves rich. Indignation and envy could easily drive us to reforming the banking system and money markets to curb these people's greed. We might end up with better bankers and less rapacious traders but there's no guarantee that we'll end up with a less dysfunctional economy. Getting rid of a flaw is a system isn't the same as making it work properly. Before we start reforming our economy we need to be clear about what we want it to do for us.

5 | Function

In the wake of the banking crisis of 2007/08 there has been a clamour of voices calling for something to be done to make sure that such catastrophe cannot happen again. Lots of people are focused on fixing the banking system – some saying that more regulation is required, others advocating a variety of structural reforms. At the same time, governments across the globe are trying to reduce national deficits and debt levels for fear of being held to ransom by the bond markets. Teams of economists and political advisors are coming up with ideas to fix the government borrowing problem, or the banking problem, or the private debt problem. Some of these ideas are being put into practice in the teeth of strong opposition from those with different ideas. Meanwhile we have a cacophony of voices from various sectors of the business community, each of which is lobbying for special measures to be taken to prop up their particular bit of the economy. History suggests that this piecemeal approach to the immediate problems of our economy is unlikely to be effective in the long run. We've been through banking crises and economic recessions before and none of the solutions that have been implemented have stopped new crises and recessions from coming along behind them. Fiddling about with solutions to fix immediate, isolated problems is folly. It's obvious to anyone who's looking beyond a particular tub to thump that there are serious flaws in the way that our economy works and unless we find a better way of managing the entirety of our economic affairs we condemn ourselves to perpetual instability and want – a regular cycle of boom and bust that's underpinned by persistent, corrosive poverty. Our economic system is ripe for reform but before we start proposing solutions we have to be clear about what we are trying to achieve. What is the purpose of our economic system? What do we want it to do for us? The first thing to understand is that the system we struggle with today was never designed to fulfil any particular function. Commerce, banking, government, and the ways that they interact have evolved over centuries in response to a tangle of human desires and fears. Business and politics have always attracted individuals on the make – people whose primary motivation is to become ever richer and more powerful – and our systems of commerce and government have always been manipulated by these people for their own advantage. Pick any time you like in history from the days of Niccolo Machiavelli to those of Rupert Murdoch and you'll find examples of people exerting influence on the ways that our society works in order to give themselves a bigger slice of cake. They haven't, of course, had it all their own way thanks to the efforts of many worthy souls who have toiled to make the world a fairer place, but the end result of these competing interests is our ridiculous, dysfunctional system in which we lurch between boom and bust with the shadows of poverty and despair always looming over us.

Our economy can be a confusing creature – a bewildering muddle of sectors, institutions, and systems that is further complicated by the language that's used to describe its workings. But at its heart the economy is simple: it's about individual needs. It's about me and you getting enough of the things that we need to sustain us – food, shelter, security, entertainment, and so on – but our economic system has never been able to deliver these most basic of outcomes to all of its participants. Too many people in the UK spend large parts of their lives in absolute poverty, unable to feed themselves properly or keep themselves warm during the winter months. Many more – perhaps the majority of us – live in fear of not being able to get enough money every month to pay the bills, and therefore live under the threat of poverty for all of our lives. Our starting point when considering how to reform our economy must be the requirement for the system to provide every man, woman and child with the means to sustain themselves regardless of their circumstances. If this is starting to sound uncomfortably utopian, fear not – I'm not about to launch into a proposal for a fantasy world where everyone agrees to share nicely and live in peace and harmony for ever, amen. Aiming for an economy in which no-one has to suffer the pain of absolute poverty isn't an argument for material equality. Some people are driven by getting and having ever-greater material wealth while others are happy with much less. Let this diversity of desire flourish while ensuring there is a minimum standard of comfortable living – a baseline prosperity – below which we will not allow anyone to fall. Some of you may have been drawn to this book hoping that I would be advocating the overthrow of the capitalist system in favour of something overtly redistributive or environmentally sustainable and will now be disappointed. Arguments over material fairness, or ecological sustainability, can only be taken so far before they hit the buffers of credibility. Human beings are creatures that have a limited appetite for sharing. Whatever our proposals are for economic reform they have to be made to work within the boundaries of human altruism. Similarly, despite the widespread recognition that environmental sustainability is a good thing, few people are ready to give up easy travel, cheap supermarket food, and recreational shopping. The changes that are needed for humanity to live equitably and sustainably on the planet are so deep and far-reaching they will take decades, perhaps centuries, to occur. In the meantime our economy will continue to malfunction, condemning too many of us to the fear or reality of poverty. Sorting out our economic system will make it easier to tackle problems of fairness and sustainability, so it's a good first step for those of you with more ambitious goals. Trying to get to where you would like us to be without first having a stable, reliable economy just isn't practical.

As we have seen, the necessities of life come to us via a vast and complex network of human endeavour. Whatever we decide to do to reform our economic system it must be designed to encourage these productive activities and make it easy for people to participate in them. Our capitalist system has had a lot of bad press in recent years, much of it well deserved. However, there is something pragmatic about allowing the appetite for personal gain to drive our productive economy. The desire for wealth and power is a strong motivator and if we don't allow people to feed that desire who is going to tackle the jobs that are difficult, dangerous and unpleasant? Many things that we take for granted are provided by the guts and determination of men and women who work in environments that most of us would not suffer for a day, let alone make a career of. There are few of us who would relish working in a mine, repairing a sewer, shovelling manure, or wrestling with frozen machinery on a drilling platform in the North Sea, but we're lucky enough to have such people among us and one of the things that drives them is the desire to capture a chunk of well-deserved spending money in return for the effort that they put in. The profit motive doesn't only encourage people to produce useful stuff through physical endeavour. The technology that makes modern life comfortable, safe and fulfilling doesn't just appear out of nowhere. The intellectual and technical effort that's required to devise a new treatment for cancer or create energy-efficient glass is considerable, as are the costs of running laboratories and workshops to produce and refine prototypes that can be turned into viable products. The people who invest time and resources in technological developments do so because they can see opportunities to get rich. Not only is capitalism good at getting things done it's also so ingrained in our culture that it would be folly to try to go against it. We need an economic environment in which productive enterprise can flourish and capitalism provides us with a familiar and effective framework in which to harness the energy, ingenuity and enthusiasm of people who are good at getting things done.

Economics, capitalism, business, productivity – they are all about change. At the most fundamental level a change in how I feel tells me that my body needs food and this provides an opportunity for someone to convert raw materials into something that I want to eat and then bargain with me to get something in return. Every commercial transaction is the result of someone wanting to change their circumstances and every industry is always changing how it does things in order to provide its customers with a better product, or to squeeze more profit out of the enterprise. The economist Joseph Schumpeter called this feature of capitalism "creative destruction" – a system that's never stationary, always moving away from what's familiar towards new (hopefully better) ways of doing things. The problem with creative destruction is the damage that it can leave in its wake. At its worst this includes environmental catastrophe, poverty and human misery. Our reformed system must provide a stable environment in which the forces of creative destruction can operate without inflicting serious collateral damage to the planet or to people who find themselves in the midst of creatively destructive events. The upheavals in our societies that are the result of the actions of men and women can be dwarfed by the effects of natural catastrophes like earthquakes, storms, drought, or disease. Our system must also be sufficiently stable to withstand the aftermath of natural disasters and provide us with a solid foundation on which a damaged society can be rebuilt.

I once heard a story about a man called Jimmy Dow who worked as a storeman for an engineering firm. Jimmy had a thing about record-keeping. His storeroom was immaculate, as were his inventories of what came in and what went out. His bosses loved him because there was never a nut, bolt or washer unaccounted for and a job was never delayed because of a shortage of components. This obsession with keeping track of things extended into Jimmy's private life. One of his many foibles was to record the serial numbers of the banknotes that he received in his wage packet and then record where he spent the notes. Occasionally, a serial number would recur – the same note would appear in his wage packet on more than one occasion. Jimmy's favourite note was one that he spent on a fish supper in the summer of 1976 on the sea front in Swanage, 600 miles from Aberdeen. This one pound note reappeared in his Christmas wage packet more than four years later. Anyone unlucky enough to be cornered by Jimmy in the pub would be regaled with the story of that one pound note, and Jimmy's speculations as to the route that it might have taken during those four and a half years from the chip shop in Dorset to his wage packet in Aberdeen. Although our modern digital money has no serial numbers that we can use to track it, it circulates just as freely as Jimmy's famous one pound note. Old Jimmy is long gone but if his grandson, Jim, paid for a fish supper in Swanage with his credit card it's logically possible to map a series of transactions over a period of time that connect the payment for the fish and chips with the digital money that's paid into Jim's bank account as salary several years later. Money flows around our economy, continually being passed from hand to hand, from account to account, making it easy for us to sell our labour, profit from our investments, and buy the things that we need. Our economy demands that we use money as a means of exchange, which means that not having money to spend renders you powerless. You might have experienced the embarrassment of arriving at the supermarket checkout with a full trolley only to discover that you've left your money at home. In that moment you are transformed from a fully-empowered participant in the business of shopping to an impotent outsider. Now imagine living with that feeling of impotence all the time. Think about how hard life would be if you never have enough money to participate in everyday life. Having money to spend is the key thing. Not having money but having money *to spend* – the distinction is important to grasp. It's the spending of money that matters, both for our personal well-being and for the health of the economy as a whole. If we don't have the money to spend we can't pay for the food in the trolley, and if we don't pay for the food then the supermarket employees and owners, and all of the people back along the chain to the farmers and their suppliers will suffer. As individuals, if we don't have money to spend every day of our lives we will very quickly be forced onto the charity of others. Collectively, if we don't have money to spend our economy will grind to a halt and there will be no charity big enough to take care of us. If money is the oxygen of an economy, spending is breathing.

However, spending is only one half of the cashflow equation. We can't spend it if we don't have it. Very few of us are given enough money at birth to last a full lifetime, so the vast majority of us rely on getting money in small but regular chunks so that we can buy the things that we need. Our culture places great emphasis on the virtue of 'earning' the money that we get and disapproves of people being given money without having 'earned' it. However, if we look at the numbers we find out that most of us get our money without 'earning' it. According to the Office for National Statistics (ONS) in January 2012 only 29.12 million people of the 63 million in the UK were in paid employment. Of these only 23.18 million were working in the private sector, the other 5.94 million being government employees. Some newspapers and many of their readers are of the opinion that the labours of these 23.18 million hardy souls in the private sector heroically support the remaining 40 million. The reality is a lot less clear cut. Some people in the private sector are doing work of questionable value to the economy as a whole, while some of the 40 million are toiling valiantly without being paid for their labour – volunteers, carers, home-makers, and the like. Most government workers are providing services that support the private sector in ways that are rarely acknowledged and without which the private sector would struggle to function. As well as non-paid workers and government employees the 40 million of so-called non-productive population includes children, the elderly, the infirm, and the idle rich, all of whom have good reasons for not being in paid employment. It also includes people who are classified as 'economically inactive', some of whom are looking for work but not claiming benefits, and some of whom are chronically workshy. Some people get some or all of their money directly from people who are in paid employment – children and home-makers being the obvious examples. Around half of the population, including many who are in paid employment, get some or all of their money in the form of government benefit payments – pensions, incapacity benefit, income support, etc. A lot of people, including those in paid employment, get some money as interest from money that's on loan to the banks, and some people live entirely off usury. The point to note is that the vast majority of people get some or all of the money that they need from sources other than paid employment. Those who wholly 'earn' their living are in the minority. The other thing to note is that many people work extremely hard for no direct monetary reward at all. There is nothing inherently virtuous about getting money in exchange for work. As discussed earlier, money is a poor measure of the value of someone's effort so placing earned income above investment income or benefits in a hierarchy of worth doesn't make any sense – they are merely different ways of distributing back to the spenders money that has been spent, so that it can be re-spent. Wages, salaries, interest payments, pensions, income support and so on are just different ways of managing the cashflow of the economy. Unfortunately none of these methods of redistributing spent money is very efficient. Around half of the population is unemployable because of age, health, or temperament so they are unable to benefit from the distribution of money via wages and salaries. Most of the population is unable to generate any significant income from usury because they don't have enough spare money to lend. This leaves government benefits as the main way in which money is cycled through the population as a whole so that it can be spent and re-spent. The problem with government benefits is that the money has to be gathered from the economy before it can be distributed and the people from whom it is gathered are somewhat reluctant to let it go. No-one likes paying taxes and people who are liable for them will do everything in their power to avoid giving what they see as 'their' money to the government. This means government is always short of money for benefits and has to be very careful how it spends what it has available. As a consequence most benefits are means tested, meaning that people have to be assessed individually to see if they are poor enough to qualify. Means testing is very complicated and expensive to administer, and results in lots of unwelcome anomalies where people who need help are denied it, and people who get help are trapped in the system. Some are unwilling to try to get out of the benefits system for fear of not being able to get back in again if times get hard, while others become culturally stuck in the system, unable to motivate themselves to do anything else. Means tested benefits, paid for by taxation, are a huge source of resentment and stigma. Many taxpayers resent having to pay for benefits, and many of the recipients hate the stigma of being 'on benefits'. From the perspective of a prosperous economy, where money needs to be available and mobile, the system of distributing spent money via taxes and benefits in order for it to be re-spent is woefully inefficient, absorbing the energies of legions of bureaucrats that could be put to productive use elsewhere in the economy, and condemning millions of people to live on the periphery of society due to lack of spending power. A primary function of our economy must be to provide everyone with a reliable flow of cash through their hands without impeding the productive economy or marginalising any particular group of people.

At the heart of our dysfunctional economic system is the tension between using money as a means of exchange and using money as a store of value. We have seen how money can make an economy work when it's available and mobile – the £50 note in our island story was all that was required to get the community trading again. We've also seen how our culture is obsessed with the idea of using stored money as a measure of wealth, how this hoarding of money causes our economy to stagnate, and how the problem is made worse by usury and speculation – using money in order to capture more money. If reform is to deliver the things that we need – baseline prosperity, productivity, stability, and cashflow – we must find a way to discourage excessive hoarding of money and encourage putting it to productive use. When we have spare money we tend to put it into a savings account at the bank, getting interest payments from the bank in return. Few of us know or care what the bank does with our money or what effect their use of it has on the economy as a whole, so let's have a closer look at this. The first thing to understand is that any money that you have in the bank, whether it's in a current account or a savings account, isn't your money. When you make a deposit into your account you give your money away. The money becomes the property of the bank and the numbers in your account are nothing more than a record of the amount of money that the bank owes you. There is a popular perception (which the banks like to promote) that the money you deposit is lent by the bank to people who want to borrow money. The idea is that your savings are lent to me for my mortgage, for which I pay a high rate of interest to the bank which pays you a smaller rate of interest for the use of your money. That would be what economists call full reserve banking and it's not how our system works. Most economists and bankers appear to believe that we use a system called fractional reserve banking where the bank is allowed to make loans up to a multiple of the value of its reserves at the central bank. For example, if a bank has £100M of reserves at the Bank of England and the reserve requirement is 10% the bank can lend a total of £900M. It does this, as explained previously, by creating the money for the loans out of thin air. Although fractional reserve banking is widely believed to be the way that our system operates it isn't really how it works at all. What actually happens is that banks lend as much as they think the market will bear and balance the books at the end of each day by juggling what they are owed by other banks with the reserves that they hold in the Bank of England. There may be a theoretical reserve requirement but in practice it's ignored. In reality there is no direct connection between the money in your savings account and the activities of the bank. Your money actually does nothing more than make the bank look a little bit bigger, which allows it to do more of whatever it thinks will be most profitable. We've seen how usury and speculation make lots of profits for the banks and do lots of damage to the economy by starving productive businesses of investment while encouraging boom-bust cycles. This means that we, as savers, are partly responsible for the harm that the banks do to our economy. The key thing to understand is that banks, because they have a monopoly of our money storage systems, are able to use our spare money for whatever purpose provides the greatest benefit for the banks. The problem with this is that what benefits the banks is often (if not always) detrimental to the economy as a whole. Our reforms must take this into account and include ways to encourage the use of spare money for productive investment while discouraging harmful usury and speculation.

In summary, if we are going to reform our dysfunctional economic system we have to make sure that we tackle the system as a whole and not just little bits of it that are in the headlines. Before we start looking at how to reform the system we have to be clear about what we want from our economy. The five things that we want our economy to do for us are:

~ encourage productive people to be productive

~ provide baseline prosperity for everybody

~ provide reliable cashflow throughout the entire economy

~ encourage investment of spare money in productive activities

~ provide a stable environment that can withstand the effects of creative destruction and natural disaster

Now that we know what we want our economic system to do for us let's have a look at how we might make it work.

6 | Five Things

Of the five things that we want our economy to do for us the most important is rewarding the energy and enthusiasm of people who are good at getting things done. Our lives depend upon the labours of people who provide us with food, fuel, shelter, transport, and security. A successful economy must allow these people to flourish, and reward them for their efforts, but it would be a mistake to think that all productive people are motivated only by money. Some people, certainly, are attracted by rewards of material wealth but for others their status in society is more important, and others are motivated by the lifestyle that accompanies their work. There are many farmers, for example, who struggle to survive under our current system but are deeply attached to the land and the farming way of life. They spend their lives on the brink of insolvency which restricts their ability to invest in their farms and improve the productivity of the agricultural sector. An economic system that provided a modest income and money to invest would be incentive enough for most small farmers to grow more high-quality food, which is exactly what we need. Some people are simply motivated by the idea of being self-employed and would love the opportunity to do something productive but lack the resources to get their venture off the ground. An economy that provided these people with enough income to survive while they get a new business up and running, along with access to investment capital, would be a great encouragement and would result in a blossoming of productive activity. All of these productive people – farmers, small business owners, and high-flying entrepreneurs – would benefit from a system that provided an independent and flexible labour force that can respond to demands for help rather than one where individuals are tied into permanent full-time jobs. Currently we want to have a permanent full-time job because we fear unemployment. We fear the humiliation and poverty associated with living off government benefits. This fear has stimulated the development of employment laws that protect the interests of the employee against callous employers and have been part of a welcome shift towards more civilized relationships between bosses and workers. The downside of these laws is that they have created a culture of dependency amongst employees to the extent that many people see their employer as a rich uncle who has a duty to look after them. In many employees' minds having the job and the security that goes with it is more important than the work that they actually do. If the fear of unemployment is removed this sense of dependency will diminish: as unemployment becomes less scary people will be less inclined to cling to a job. Everyone will have more freedom to choose when to work and employers will be able to have more flexible relationships with their workforce, getting people in when there's work to be done and letting them stay away during the slack times. All of the people who are good at getting things done – whether they are self-employed, employers or employees - will also be far more motivated if a smaller proportion of their financial rewards end up in the coffers of the taxman. Providing both of these things - a basic income for productive people and lower taxes would certainly give them the encouragement they need to be productive, but the two things appear to be mutually exclusive. The basic income can only be paid for by higher taxes, surely? Before we tackle this conundrum let's look at the second thing on our list: baseline prosperity for all. We could meet this requirement by extending to everyone else the basic income that we want to provide for productive people – a regular income for everyone that covers basic living expenses.

The idea of a universal guaranteed income has been proposed in a variety of guises over many decades, often under the name of a 'citizens' income'. It's an attractive concept because it eliminates the need for means testing of government benefits, along with the socially corrosive resentment and stigma of taxpayers and benefit recipients: if everyone gets the same amount of money regardless of their circumstances there can be no legitimate complaints about fairness. The problem with a universal benefit is the cost. I have attempted to calculate the cost of giving everyone in the UK a basic income of £12,000 a year and my best estimate suggests that funding this through taxation would require an 90% increase in annual tax revenues from their current levels. There are good arguments that such punitive tax rates would discourage productive activity – stop people from bothering to do all of the things that we need to do to sustain ourselves – but such arguments pale into insignificance when compared to the resistance of taxpayers to the idea of paying more tax. The working population, the business community, and consumers are never going to agree to a 90% increase in annual taxation. We hate having to pay taxes at their current rates. We think of the money that we get (from whatever source) as ***our*** money and we resent the government taking any of it away from us. Funding a universal income from conventional taxation is a non-starter but we may be able to learn something from the tax and benefit system that will help us to find a way to make a universal income work.

Most people who receive benefits are so short of money that they have to spend everything that they get every month, so benefit money goes quickly and directly from the benefit recipients into the general economy. The flow of money from the economy back to the benefit recipients via the government is much slower thanks to our complicated tax system, but we could say that the same money flows round and round indefinitely from recipients to the economy to government and back to recipients. The cycle suffers, however, from a major problem. The route that the benefit money has to travel through the government part of the system is tortuous. Governments are under tremendous pressure to use taxpayers money wisely, which means that a great deal of bureaucratic effort goes into monitoring and justifying the payment of benefits. Governments are also susceptible to persuasion and coercion from special interest groups who lobby for taxes to be spent on their particular thing, which often means that one group of beneficiaries is favoured over others. The layers of administration that are required to satisfy these many and varied demands reduces the efficiency of the system. Money is absorbed and evaporated by the machinery of government, so less of it is available for distributing as benefits, and people whose need is immediate are left wanting. Our tax-and-benefits system is a cyclical cashflow but it's very cumbersome and inefficient. The ways in which we collect taxes are bewilderingly complicated and the timescales for collection and distribution of the money don't fit comfortably with the way that the money is spent by the benefit recipients. The whole system is a mess that costs huge amounts of money to administer and causes huge amounts of resentment from just about every part of our society. There must be a better way.

Thinking of a universal income in terms of a cashflow cycle instead of a constant linear spend is a step in the right direction. If we look at it in linear terms an annual income of £12,000 for everyone in the UK would cost around £720,000M a year, or £7,200,000M over the course of a decade. The numbers are horribly huge, so let's get rid of the word 'cost' and think in terms of cashflow. Instead of spending £720,000M every year let's think about a single chunk of money moving in a continual cycle from the general economy into our hands to pay for our basic needs, which we spend back into the general economy. Looking at it this way, it's obvious that the period of the cycle doesn't have to be as long as a year. Our basic needs of food, housing, fuel, etc. tend to be paid for by the week or the month, not annually, so let's reduce the period of the cycle from a year to a month. This means that the amount of money that we need is reduced to £1,000 for each person – a total of around £60,000M. This is less than 12% of the annual tax revenue of the government and only 2.5% of the total amount of money sloshing about in the economy. Not only does £60,000M feel like a manageable number, we only have to find it once – the same £60,000M can be recycled through the economy month after month, year after year, ad infinitum. If we think of a universal income in terms of a monthly cashflow cycle the concept starts to look like it might be viable.

If everyone is given enough money every month to enjoy a basic level of prosperity the vast majority of government benefits will be redundant. The universal income will replace all of the benefits that are paid to people for normal living expenses which total c.£188,000M a year. It will also eliminate the need for a range of tax credits and allowances that cost the exchequer c.£85,000M a year. So a universal benefit would reduce government expenditure by a total of c.£273,000M each year. If we abolish National Insurance Contributions (employer's and employee's) and VAT we'll reduce government revenue by c.£200,000M a year, which still leaves us with a surplus of c.£73,000M a year to play with, which we could use to reduce the deficit (the amount that the government has to borrow each year). We'll discuss these opportunities in more detail in later chapters but we can see that as well as providing baseline prosperity for everyone in the country our universal income can eliminate some of the taxes that discourage economic activity, thereby rewarding our productive people for their efforts. Another tick against the first item on our list of five essential functions for our new system.

All of this sounds wonderful but we mustn't forget the £60,000M that we need to cycle through the economy every month so that everyone gets their £1,000 of universal income. How are we going to make that work? Let's imagine the £60,000M starts the cycle as a single pot of money in a 'citizens' bank'. On the first day of each month £1,000 is transferred from this pot of money into an account that's been set up in your name at the citizens' bank. There are only two restrictions on what you do with this money. Firstly, you can't withdraw it directly as cash. Secondly, if any of the money remains in your citizen's account at the end of the month, it disappears – use it or lose it. You can transfer this money into your normal bank account or you can use it to pay for stuff directly from your citizen's account via a debit card or internet banking. As soon as it's been transferred (or spent) into the normal banking system the universal income money behaves exactly the same as all the other money in the economy – it's impossible to tell which is which. That's the first half of the cycle taken care of, but how do we get the £60,000M back into the citizens' bank ready to be shared out again at the beginning of the following month? We don't know exactly where the £60,000M has been spent but we do know that it's c.2.5% of the £2,300,000M of electronic money that's sloshing around our economy. The beauty of electronic money (as opposed to notes and coins) is that it's very easy to move it automatically using the power of computers. This means that we can collect 2.5p off every pound every month to replenish the £60,000M universal income pot so that it can be shared out again at the beginning of the following month. Recycling a small percentage of the UK money supply every month guarantees basic prosperity for everyone, replaces a substantial chunk of the inefficient tax-and-benefit system, and encourages productive people to be productive. It also does something very interesting to the nature of money.

If the value of money in the bank is being eroded at a rate of 2.5% per month money can no longer be used as a long term store of value. If you have £1,000 in your account at the start of the month you'll only have around £975 left by the end of the month. By the end of the year you'll only have £740 left. The system for recycling the universal income money means that money can no longer be left lying idle in the bank and retain its value. Idle money will always lose value. For a culture that's obsessed by measuring wealth in terms of stored money this is a very difficult concept to grasp but let's look and see what the effects will be on the economy as a whole. If money in the bank is constantly losing value there is a big incentive to spend it on something that is of real value rather than ascribing value to the money itself. This reinforces the notion, as discussed earlier, of money only being truly valuable at the moment at which we spend it. The pressure to spend will encourage some people to use all of their available money every month, which will ensure demand for goods and services. This means that there will be lots of opportunities for energetic people to do productive things, which will provide lots of jobs for people who like to be employed. The pressure to spend money, along with the distribution of £60,000M every month among everyone in the country will ensure that our new system delivers the third essential function on our list – reliable cashflow distributed widely throughout the economy. Some people will struggle to spend all their money every month, either because they have more than they know what to do with or their natures are more prudent than profligate. These people will prefer to put their money to work by investing it. The interesting thing about our new system is that if we try to 'invest' our money by gambling on the prices of financial assets it will always be eroded by 2.5% per month. This will act as a disincentive to trying to 'make money' out of manipulating money. The rewards of successful money manipulation will effectively be taxed at a rate of 26% per annum and the costs of unsuccessful money manipulation will be increased by the same amount. The best way to avoid this will be to invest money in something where it gets spent on goods and services that are employed to generate profits – investment in the productive economy. This feature of the system delivers the fourth thing on our list, ensuring lots of money is available for investing in productive activities.

The fifth thing on our list is a stable environment that can withstand the forces of creative destruction as well as the forces of nature. Everywhere is susceptible to catastrophic events. It might be collapse of the banking system, an influenza epidemic, or an earthquake. During such times many people are unable to continue with their normal economic activities and have to rely on support from the state. We've already seen how cumbersome the benefits system is to administer. It's not designed to cope with large numbers of people requiring help all at the same time, so in times of catastrophe the government is obliged to spend heavily and inefficiently to solve immediate welfare problems, and then work out how to pay for it later. A universal income will mean that the funding of basic welfare for everyone in the country is already in place before any catastrophe comes along, be it physical or economic. In less apocalyptic times the universal income will provide a welcome degree of stability for individuals and businesses that produce the things we need. No matter what the rest of the economy is doing a guaranteed cashflow of £60,000M through the economy every month will provide a solid foundation for other economic activity. However, this will do little to cure the problem of cyclical boom and bust.

As we've seen, boom-bust cycles are the result of our money supply being determined by the appetite of private profit-making organisations (banks) to lend money. The banks see a profitable opportunity and go on a lending spree (the boom), the consequence of which is a period where the loans are repaid and the economy is progressively starved of money for general commerce (the bust). Over the last few years a lot of people have applied themselves to this problem and have come up with a variety of solutions. One of the most promising set of proposals for disconnecting the profit-making activities of the banks from determining the quantity and velocity of money in the economy comes from a group called Positive Money whose ideas are based on the work of Irving Fisher (and others) in the 1930s and more recently that of James Robertson and Joseph Huber. They propose changing the rules of banking so that banks are no longer allowed to create deposits (the numbers in your bank account) when making loans. Instead the proposal is that banks are only allowed to make loans using money that already exists. This is what's known as full reserve banking and it probably doesn't sound very radical if, like me, you used to believe that that's how bank lending actually worked. Under this system the amount of money in the economy will no longer be decided on the whim of the banks. Instead, Positive Money proposes giving control of the money supply to an independent group of people (the Money Creation Committee or MCC) whose job it will be to ensure that the economy has the right amount of money in it to keep it running sweetly. It's unlikely that this group of wise men and women will get their sums right all of the time but even if they're a few percentage points out every now and again they are far more likely to keep the money supply within a sensible range for the economy as a whole than the bankers whose influence on the money supply is driven by unabashed self-interest. The result of this change will be far smaller fluctuations in the amount of money available for general commerce, which can only increase the stability of our economic environment.

Later on I'll explain the details of how Positive Money proposes that we manage this new full reserve banking system but at its heart is a change in the way that our money is accounted for when it's in the bank. At the moment all of the money that you think you have in the bank, whether it's in a current account or a savings account, actually belongs to the bank, and when the bank goes bust you lose the lot unless the government is kind enough to replace it for you (which the UK government does for deposits up to a certain value, paid for by the taxpayer). Under the new system all of the money that you have in a current account (which Positive Money calls a 'transaction account') will remain your property and will actually be held in the Bank of England. Your bank will merely be providing you with a payment system for managing your own money. If your bank goes belly-up your money is safe and you can get access to it as soon as your account has been transferred from the dud bank to a good one. This will provide our economy with a stable system for making and receiving payments regardless of the health of the banks on the high street, and ensure that people have a safe place to keep the money that they need for general living expenses.

The money in your savings account (which Positive Money calls an 'investment account') will belong to the bank in the same way that it does now. The difference will be that you'll have to commit to keeping it in the account for a fixed period of time, or you'll have to give a few weeks' notice before you can withdraw it. This will allow the banks to manage their cashflow and (hopefully) reduce the chances of a bank being caught short of cash, which will further enhance the stability of the economy. Another significant difference is that the money that you give to the bank for investment will not be guaranteed by the government or anyone else apart from the bank. So instead of being engaged in usury as is currently the case you will be an investor sharing the risks and rewards with the bank. This means that the bank will have to work hard to convince people to put their money into an investment account and therefore there will be less opportunity for the banks to make reckless loans, which will reduce the opportunities to fund asset bubbles (e.g. housing), which will reduce the chances of booms and busts.

There are concerns about this feature of the Positive Money proposals, which I share. It's possible that most of us will choose to keep all of our money safely in transaction accounts (earning zero interest) rather than risk giving it to the banks in the hope that they will use it wisely and give us the share of the profits it generates. If this happens businesses will be starved of money to invest in new ventures or to fund gaps in cashflow, both of which are essential for a thriving productive economy. There is also nothing in Positive Money's proposals that encourages the banks to invest our spare money in the productive economy rather than use it for speculative money manipulation. However, if we combine Positive Money's proposals for reform of the banking system with the concept of recycling the universal income we provide strong incentives to put money to productive use. The choice is to hoard your money in a transaction account and see it disappear at the rate of 2.5% per month or to give it to someone else to spend on something profitable and get a share of the profits in return. If you give it to the bank to invest on your behalf it's unlikely that the bank is going to use it for gambling because, as discussed earlier, much financial speculation involves holding the money that's backing the gamble in a bank account where it's liable for the 2.5% monthly payback to the universal income pot. This means that investing in the productive economy – where the money gets spent on goods and services that are used for something profitable – will be the most attractive option for making use of spare money. The productive economy will always be well-supplied with investment capital, which will reduce the chances of recessions and increase the opportunities for new, more productive business ideas to replace old inefficient ones.

It looks as though these two ideas – a continuously cycling fund providing a guaranteed basic income for everyone, and reform of the way that our banking system is organised – will provide us with the five things that we need from our economy: rewards for people who are good at getting things done; basic prosperity for everyone; reliable cashflow throughout the economy; investment in productive activities; and a stable economic environment. Before we try to tackle any of the many queries and concerns that these concepts might raise, let's have a closer look at the detail of how they might be put into practice.

7 | Common Cashflow Fund

The idea of continuously recycling money through the economy to provide everyone with a regular income that covers their basic living costs appears to be worth investigating. Before we go any further we should give the idea a name. It's going to be a pot of money that's owned by all of us in equal share – a fund that's held in common and constantly recycled to provide each of us with our basic monthly cashflow. So let's call it the Common Cashflow Fund, or CCF.

In the previous chapter I suggested that £1,000 a month is what each of us needs to cover our basic living expenses, but how realistic is that amount? The Joseph Rowntree Foundation (JRF) has researched this very subject and concluded that (in 2012) a single adult needed to spend £1,135/month in order to meet what they call a Minimum Income Standard (MIS). A lone parent with one child needs £2,180/month and a couple with two children need £2,968/month to enjoy a similar standard of living. The MIS includes the costs of running a car, which the compilers of the report argue is essential for families with children, and some other items that many people would not regard as basic necessities. My own experience suggests that a single person can live in reasonable comfort on about £800/month, while a couple with a two children need around £1,700/month for a similar standard of living, so the JRT figures might be a bit high, but costs vary throughout the country and there doesn't seem to be any virtue in being mean with the CCF shares. Remember that many people will have to live off their CFF monthly share for decades because of old age or infirmity so the value of the shares should be generous enough to allow these people to enjoy life without having to worry about paying the basic bills. However, care must be taken to keep the total value of the CCF at a level where the payback rate doesn't inhibit the productive economy. The trick will be to find the right balance. Using the JRF figures as a guide it seems reasonable to suggest that our monthly guaranteed income rates should be as follows: £1,000/month for each adult; £800/month for an only child; £450/month for every child who has one or more siblings under the age of 16. These amounts add up to a little bit less than the JRF figures but reductions in tax that will accompany the CCF means that the cost of living will probably fall significantly, which should more than make up the difference. In reality it would be sensible to develop a formula to work out how much the monthly shares should be, taking into account all of the things that we need to live a life of basic comfort and security. In the meantime, for the purposes of our discussion, £1,000 per adult, £800 per only child, and £450 for children with siblings under 16 years old will be accurate enough. So, assuming these individual monthly payments, what's the total amount of money that we need for the Common Cashflow Fund? There are approximately 49 million adults in the UK, 3.7 million single children, and 9.9 million children in families with one or more brother or sister under the age of 16. So the total amount of money that we would need to recycle every month would be c.£57,000M, a bit less than the £60,000M guesstimate that we came up with earlier.

We now have to decide where the CCF money should come from. £57,000M is a substantial chunk of cash and the only realistic sources are the government or the Bank of England. The CCF will replace a long list of benefits that are currently paid out by the government so it might sound sensible to use this benefit money to create the CCF. It's unlikely, however, that the Treasury's own cashflow could cope with a single payment of £57,000M on the first day of the month that the was chosen for the start of the CCF system. More importantly there is a strong argument for keeping the universal cashflow scheme completely separate from government. Elected politicians are constantly buffeted by events and lobbied by special interest groups which means they are not always able or willing to do what is in the best interests of everyone. Government should not, therefore, have any control, direct or indirect, over the CCF. That leaves us with the Bank of England, which is already somewhat independent of government and would seem to be ideally placed to establish the CCF and administer it on our behalf. This would save the trouble and expense of setting up a 'citizens' bank'. The first thing the Bank of England would have to do is create a central CCF account and credit that account with £57,000M of digital money. The Bank could create this digital money out of nothing but there's already a source of money in the economy which provides a much neater solution for the initial financing of the Common Cashflow Fund. More of which later.

For now let's assume that we have our CCF money, £57,000M of it, sitting in a big (digital) pot in the Bank of England. The next thing we need is for the Bank of England to create individual CCF bank accounts for every citizen of the UK. This might sound like a huge and expensive task but each of us already has a unique personal account number within the National Insurance system. These National Insurance Numbers can be used to create individual CCF bank accounts for every man, woman and child who is a UK citizen. On the first day of the month each adult's CCF account will be credited with their £1,000 plus the CCF share of any children in their care. As adults our CCF account comes with a debit card so that we can use our CCF money to pay for stuff wherever card payments are accepted. We can also transfer money from our CCF account to our normal bank account by using our card at any Post Office, or via internet banking, which can also be used for online payments.

There are three main differences between our CCF account and an ordinary bank account. Firstly, we can't withdraw our CCF money as cash. Secondly, we can't pay any money into our CCF account (only the Bank of England can do that). Thirdly, the money that's paid into our CCF account at the start of every month has a shelf life: it has to be spent within a month. On the last day of every month any money that's left in an individual CCF account is automatically put back into the CCF pot, ready to be shared out again the next day – the first day of the following month. This 'use it or lose it' feature of the system is designed to encourage people to spend their monthly share, ensuring that most of the money moves steadily through the first half of the cycle, from our CCF accounts into the economy.

Let's now look at how the other half of the cycle might work – CCF money moving from the economy back into the CCF pot every month. Most of the UK's money supply – more than 97% of it – is held in the accounts of financial institutions as electronic records, to which the CCF money will be added every month as we spend it out of our CCF accounts. Thanks to the power of computers it's technically feasible to take a little bit of money from every bank account every month and return this money to the CCF. Taking £57,000M from the banking system in a lump sum at the end of each month probably isn't a good idea. It would cause a big dip in the money supply which might be disruptive to the economy. A single monthly CCF repayment might also provide dishonest people with opportunities for hiding money from the CCF payback system. A more continuous flow of money from the economy back into the CCF pot feels like a more sensible proposition. If the money is recovered on an hourly basis the flow of money out of the economy into the CCF pot is more likely to match the flow of money out of our individual CCF accounts and into the economy, and it makes it much harder to hide money from the payback system. So every hour all the money held in any electronic form in any financial institution is reduced by the CCF hourly payback rate. The money is transferred from the banks to the CCF pot in the Bank of England hour after hour, a little bit at a time. By the end of the month all of the CCF money has been recovered and the pot is full, ready to be shared out again.

The problem with this electronic payback system is that it won't work with notes and coins. There is no way of shaving off a percentage of the value of a £20 note every hour when it's tucked away in your pocket. So what's to be done? One option would be to leave notes and coins outside the CCF system altogether, but this would create a haven where people could shelter their money from CCF payback. For example, in January you could transfer your CCF share into your bank account, withdraw the £1,000 as cash and stuff it under your mattress. If you did the same thing every month for a year you'd have £12,000 of CCF money which the payback system couldn't touch. If lots of people copied you we would soon run out of notes and coins for everyday transactions and we'd have to increase the CCF payback rate to make up for the hidden money. Hiding money from CCF payback would be dishonest – equivalent to stealing from our friends and neighbours – but for some people the opportunity to cheat would be too attractive to resist. Another option would be to create some sort of accounting system that tracked notes and coins through the economy and removed the CCF share whenever the currency passed through a business or a bank. Inevitably there would be scope for fraud and avoidance, but even if the system was built so that the leaks were minimal the administrative burden on businesses and banks would be very unpopular. The third option is to abolish notes and coins altogether, replacing them with electronic cash systems. Such systems are already popular in other parts of the world and are starting to gain a toehold in the UK. These use a card or a mobile phone to make small payments without having to enter a PIN number or sign a bit of paper. Payments are quicker to make than using notes and coins because there's no need to give change, and the system is more secure than carrying cash because the money can't be lost or stolen. The beauty of this option is that it turns all money into digital money which can be accessed by the CCF payback system. In time, it's likely that most of us will be using these electronic cash systems in preference to notes and coins for most of our small transactions, but until this happens organically many people will be outraged at the suggestion of abolishing their beloved bank notes. One way to get around this resistance would be to use the value of the notes and coins in the economy to provide initial finance for the Common Cashflow Fund. If the Bank of England's notes were seen to be directly funding the CCF it might make the sacrifice of paper currency more bearable. If the choice is between one or the other, what would you prefer, £1,000 a month for the rest of your life or the pleasure of handling £20 notes when you go shopping? Assuming that most of us would opt for £1,000 a month, let's have a look at how it might work. We have approximately £60,000M worth of notes and coins in the UK economy, a number that conveniently accommodates the £57,000M that we need for the CCF. Notes and coins would be phased out over a period of months while the electronic cash systems were being installed and promoted. There would be a cut-off date when notes and coins were no longer legal tender. In the months leading up to this date we'd take our notes and coins to the bank where we'd convert them into digital money in our bank accounts. The banks would sell the notes and coins to the Bank of England, converting them into digital money in the banks' own accounts. The Bank of England would destroy the notes and coins, replacing them with digital money in the CCF pot. This appears to provide a neat solution to finding the money for the CCF while overcoming the problem of applying the payback system to notes and coins. How the payback system will affect what we do with our spare money, and how we'll feel about it, is worth investigating.

8 | Payback Effects

The CCF payback system will fundamentally change the way that we think about money, and what we do with our spare money. At the moment we want to hold onto as much money as possible because we think that money is the same thing as wealth. In previous chapters we've discovered that this is nonsense, that the value ascribed to money is unreliable and hoarded money merely gives us the illusion of wealth. Under the CCF payback system the delusion that money is a reliable store of wealth will disappear and we will have to balance the convenience of holding spare money for future spending with the inconvenience of losing a little bit of it every hour to the Common Cashflow Fund. How we achieve this balance will depend on our individual circumstances. For someone who has no spare money and whose only income is from the CCF, the payback system will have no direct effect: they'll pay for their living expenses out of their CCF account and that money will be collected from other people's accounts and returned to the CCF each month. But how will it work for the rest of us?

At the time of writing there's about £2,250,000M of digital money in the UK economy. If we add £57,000M that we've converted from notes and coins into digital money for the CCF we get a total money supply of c.£2,307,000M, all in digital format. On average, there are 730 hours in a month, which means that around £78M has to be recovered every hour to replenish the CCF pot with £57,000M every month. This gives us an hourly payback rate of 0.0034%. So every hour about a third of a penny will be taken from every pound that's held by every financial institution and automatically sent to the CCF pot at the Bank of England. This will happen continuously, every hour of every day. How will this affect the money in your bank account?

Let's suppose that we've reformed the banking system along the lines proposed by Positive Money. Instead of a current account in which 'your money' was actually owned by the bank you now have a transaction account and the money that's in it is owned by you. This means that every hour of every day the amount of money that you have in your transaction account is being reduced at a rate of 0.0034%. If you have £1,000 in the account at midnight on Monday it will have been reduced to £999.33 by midnight on Tuesday. Losing £0.77 doesn't sound too bad, but remember it happens every day of the year. If you leave £1,000 in your account for 365 days you'll lose c.£255 to the CCF payback system, which doesn't sound very attractive at all. But fear not, there are several things that we can do to prevent our spare money from disappearing into the CCF pot. Firstly, we can compensate for CCF payback erosion by using our CCF monthly share to maintain a store of money in our transaction accounts. If I have £4,300 in my transaction account at the start of the month, the CCF payback rate of 0.0034% per hour means that it will have shrunk by around

£100 by the end of the month, leaving me with £4,200. But as well as taking away £100 the CCF gives me £1,000 every month. If I use some of my CCF share every month to replace the £100 that has been taken away by the payback system I can keep my £4,300 safely in my transaction account and still have £900 to spend. In fact, if I have enough income from other sources and can afford to use all of my £1,000 CCF share to replace the payback from my transaction account I can maintain a balance of around £48,000. By using all of their CCF shares every month a couple can keep c.£96,000 safe and secure in their transaction account, while a family of four can maintain a balance of c.£137,000.

For most people who spend the majority of their income and are happy to keep only a few thousand pounds in the bank for emergencies the give-and-take of the CCF works very well. But for someone with considerably more than £48,000 of savings the Common Cashflow Fund might sound like an attack on their personal wealth. If I have £100,000 in the bank on the 1st of September the CCF will have taken away c.£2,300 of it by the 1st of October. OK, I'll have received £1,000 from the CCF but that still leaves me £1,300 worse off. However, this loss is compensated to an extent by the abolition of national insurance contributions and VAT. Depending on how much I earn and how much I spend every month the abolition of these taxes could leave me with additional disposable income that amounts to more than the £1,300 that's lost to the CCF payback system. Of course, if my stash of money is £400,000 and my income is only £2,000 a month, the sums aren't going to add up, which will force me to do something with my hoard of money instead of leaving it rotting in the bank. This is the beauty of the CCF payback system – it allows all of us to hoard an amount of money that's in proportion to our income but discourages us from hoarding too much, motivating us to release the money into the economy, which is exactly what an economy needs in order for it to thrive. An unlimited amount of money can be kept safely in a transaction account as long as the owner has sufficient income to match the monthly CCF payback for which the stash of money is liable, but in the long term using spare income to maintain the value of a large hoard of stagnant money doesn't make sense. There are better ways of preventing the value of our money being eroded by the CCF payback system. Spending it, for example.

We've already seen that money only has any real value at the moment that you exchange it for something that's useful or desirable. The CCF payback system reinforces this truism and encourages people to spend rather than hoard. Some people will choose to spend their money on a more comfortable lifestyle – buying more expensive food and drink, for example. Others will prefer to convert their money into material goods that are regarded as good stores of value, like gold or works of art, or home improvements. Creative entrepreneurs will doubtless dream up lots of new products – ephemeral and durable – to tempt people to part with their money. All of these products, no matter how sensible or frivolous, will require the efforts of lots of people to bring them to the market, which means lots of jobs, which means lots of wages and salaries, which means lots of money moving through the economy. Money will be available and mobile, exactly what an economy needs in order to thrive.

The third option that we have for protecting our spare money from erosion by the CCF payback system is to invest it in activities that are profitable. We can do this directly, by investing in a business venture that we think will produce a healthy profit stream, or we can give our money to someone to invest on our behalf, typically via some sort of savings account at a bank. We've already seen that the money in your savings account is actually the property of the bank. The 'money' that you see on the your bank statement is nothing more than a promise from the bank to repay you this amount at a later date. The investment accounts that are being proposed by Positive Money will be exactly the same as a savings account in this respect – you will give the money to the bank to invest on your behalf and the bank will give you a contract saying when it will repay the original sum of money along with your share of the profits that it has earned. Because the money in the investment account belongs to the bank, the bank is liable for the CCF payback. So when you transfer £10,000 from your transaction account to your investment account ownership of the money is transferred from you to the bank and it's the bank that takes the hit of £7.75/day being repaid to the CCF. This means that, whatever else they do with your money, the bankers certainly won't leave it sitting idle. The CCF payback system will put pressure on the banks to invest the money promptly. As discussed previously, the other thing that the banks will be less inclined to do is speculate. Using our investment money to gamble on movements in the prices of assets will no longer be such an attractive activity because all of the money involved will be subject to the CCF payback system, which is equivalent to paying tax at an annual rate of c.25.5%. Instead the banks will be keen to invest our money in projects and businesses where the money is exchanged for materials, wages, and overheads that are used to produce something that will generate a profitable income. Doubtless some of this investment will go to fund things that are of little value to the sum of human happiness but a lot of it will be directed towards activities that provide people with the things that they need to sustain them or make their lives more comfortable or fulfilling. The pressure on the banks to invest the money instead of speculating with it means that businesses are unlikely to be starved of funds as is commonly the case under our current system. Some of the profits that are generated by these productive activities will be given to the bank as a return on its investment in the venture, some of which the bank will give to us as a return on our investment in the bank. We can use this income to protect a larger hoard of money in our transaction account, or we can spend it, or we can re-invest it.

How we make ourselves feel wealthy under the CCF payback system might change significantly, but then again it might not change very much at all. At the time of writing the real rate of inflation is higher than typical savings account interest rates. People who currently have money in the bank are seeing the value of their hoard drop every month. Institutional investors are buying government bonds with yields that are often less than the rate of inflation. These individuals and institutions are effectively paying banks and governments to keep their money safe. For those of us who live hand-to-mouth every month it's difficult to understand why anyone would choose to let their wealth be eroded in such a way. However, if your annual income is greater than your annual spending, and this surplus is greater than the amount that's being lost to inflation you're still becoming wealthier every year. Your priority is to make sure your overall position of wealth is secure and you're quite happy to use some of your spare money to maintain that security. The money in the bank or the bonds is as safe as money can possibly be so that's where you leave it, despite the cost. The same logic will apply under the CCF payback system. People may choose to use some of their income to protect the value of a hoard of money in a transaction account. Under the CCF system income becomes more powerful than savings. It's possible that maintaining a big hoard of money will become an indicator of serious income – "she can *afford* to keep a million pounds in the bank" might be said with awe and envy instead of "she *has* a million pounds in the bank" – shifting perceptions of wealth away from the size of the pile of money that you have and concentrating instead on how much money flows through your hands.

It's equally possible that measures of wealth will shift away from hoarded money towards material possessions, which have always been used to gauge how rich someone is. This shift from cash to assets could cause spikes in the prices of things that have traditionally been seen as good stores of value – works of art, precious metals, houses, and land. Apart from the issue of public access there's very little downside to increased prices for aesthetic goods like works of art, and it might be very good indeed for working artists and their dealers. The same could be said for the likes of gold and silver which are mainly traded for their aesthetic or perceived value rather than their practical value (the exception being some goods like electronics, which may see a rise in manufacturing costs). Any increase in the price of precious metals will be good for miners, refiners, goldsmiths and the like. A spike in the values of houses and land might be more problematic if it affected the lower end of the housing market. Housing is a necessity that must be affordable for everyone. If the price of ordinary houses is pushed up by rich people looking for something to do with their spare money this will tend to push up monthly mortgage repayments and rents. This isn't just a bad deal for people who are living off their CCF monthly share, it's also a bad deal for the economy as a whole. The value of the individual CCF share is determined by a formula that includes housing costs. If housing costs rise, so will the CCF monthly share, which means that the CCF payback rate will have to increase. An increase in the CCF payback rate could easily push rich people to use more of their spare money to invest in property, which would further increase housing costs, which would trigger a further increase in the CCF – a classic example of an asset bubble causing trouble in an economy. Where a necessity like housing is in danger of becoming the focus of an investment bubble there is a strong argument for using some sort of control mechanism to stop prices from rising. In the case of houses, sales of which are already regulated, this would be relatively easy to achieve. Currently, every house that is put on the market has to have an up to date home report, which is prepared by a chartered surveyor. In the home report the surveyor includes two valuations. One is for insurance purposes and is an estimate of the cost of rebuilding the property from scratch. The other is a market value – how much the surveyor thinks the house might sell for in the current market. At the height of the last housing boom it wasn't unusual for the insurance value to be considerably less than the market value whereas after the bubble burst the market value in some locations is less than half the insurance value. If we standardised the way in which the insurance value is calculated so that it's consistent across the country and reflects realistic costs of construction we would then have a baseline that we could use to discourage speculative inflation of house prices. For example, we could use the insurance value as the legal maximum value for mortgage purposes, making it illegal to provide a mortgage for the property if the purchase price exceeded the insurance valuation. This would prevent banks from inflating house prices through mortgage lending. We could also make it illegal to charge annual rent in excess of a certain percentage of the insurance value of the property. For example, if the ceiling was set at 5% the landlord of a flat with an insurance value of £150,000 would not be allowed to charge more than £7,500 a year or £625 a month. These two bits of legislation would tie monthly housing costs to construction costs and go a long way to preventing banks and people with lots of spare money from inflating the price of housing. Using the insurance value as the maximum price for a mortgage-backed purchase prevents house prices from being driven up by speculation but allows home owners to increase the value of their property by improving or extending it – a larger or upgraded house will be given a higher insurance value. So people can still 'make money' from property but only through the application of labour and materials which increase its absolute value, unlike a typical housing boom where the market value is driven up by the availability of cheap finance.

Under the CCF system it's possible that the main measure of an individual's wealth will be the value of their investments. Hoarding money in the bank will cost money, and material assets are the subject of fashion and whim which makes them unreliable stores of value, so both of these have limited appeal. The scope for profiting from commercial activities, however, is limited only by the imagination of entrepreneurs and the appetite of buyers to spend money on products and experiences, an appetite that will be stimulated by the CCF monthly shares – money that has to be spent every month – and the CCF payback system, which discourages the hoarding of money. Businesses will need money to develop new products and services to feed this appetite so there will be lots of opportunities for people to invest their spare money and get a share of the profits. Some people will choose to take these profits as income that they will then spend, while others will choose to reinvest the profits. The size of someone's investment portfolio and the value of the income stream that it generates will probably become the main measure of personal wealth. It will still be quantified in terms of money but it will be expressed as what someone's annual investment income is rather than how much money they have. Our understanding of the value of money will have changed. Money will be valuable only when it's put to work, doing something productive. Idle money will be seen as wasteful.

So far we've been considering the effects of the CCF payback system on the internal economy of the UK, but what about international trade and currency exchange? When someone in the UK buys stuff from another country we tend to think of the money that's been spent as 'leaving the country'. If this was true it might be very difficult to collect the CCF payback from this money and it might give dishonest people a way of avoiding the CCF payback system altogether. Thankfully, that's not how our foreign exchange system works. Let's say I go on holiday to Florida with my RBS bank card, which I use to withdraw $300 from a Citibank ATM. When I get home and look at my bank statement it shows this transaction as a £195 withdrawal from my RBS account. If you think this means that I removed £195 from the UK money supply and added it into the US money supply you'd be wrong. The $300 that I got out of the ATM in Florida was given to me by Citibank.

The record of the $300 withdrawal was sent by Citibank to RBS, which triggered a transfer of $300 from RBS's dollar account to Citibank's dollar account. Meanwhile RBS took £195 out of my account to compensate itself for the $300 it gave to Citibank. The £195 remains in the UK economy – it has simply moved from my account to RBS's account where it's still liable for CCF payback. Let's reverse the direction of the exchange and make it a much larger amount of money to see how that works. Omnicorp Inc. in California decides to invest $10M in Widget Ltd. in the UK. The transaction begins with Citibank in California taking $10M from Omnicorp's account and putting it into Citbank's own account. Citibank, having agreed an exchange rate of 1.55 dollars to a pound, transfers £6.45M from its sterling account to RBS's sterling account. RBS completes the transaction by adding £6.45M to Widget's account. It might look like we've just added £6.45M to the UK money supply, but we haven't. The £6.45M was liable for CCF payback when it was in Citibank's sterling account and remains liable when it has been transferred to RBS's sterling account. While there will be no change in the mechanisms of foreign exchange the persistent loss of value due to CCF payback may result in international banks refusing to hold large reserves of sterling and/or charging customers higher fees for handling foreign exchange transactions. However, the ingenuity of bankers suggests that they will find clever ways of managing foreign exchange transactions to minimise the effects of CCF payback. Those who succeed in this regard will be able to offer their clients lower fees and will attract more foreign exchange business than their rivals.

The effect of the CCF payback system on foreign exchange rates is hard to predict. On the one hand, no-one will be keen to use sterling as a store of value, which means that banks and wealthy individuals may try to convert large quantities into foreign currencies, which will tend to lower the value of sterling on the foreign exchange markets. On the other hand, the low-tax high-investment UK economy will be very vibrant which will attract investors who will have to buy sterling in order to get a slice of the action, which will raise its value. The only certainty is that currency speculators will generally avoid buying sterling because CCF payback will act as a significant tax on any profits they might make on movements in the value of the currency. In the unlikely event of sterling becoming so hard to sell that it hinders international trade the Bank of England can enter the foreign exchange market as a guaranteed purchaser of sterling at a stable rate of exchange for UK importers (who are trying to buy goods from overseas) and international investors (who are trying to move profits abroad).

The success of the Common Cashflow Fund and the effects that it has on the economy and our perceptions of money and wealth depends to a great extent on reform of the banking system, so let's have a look at this in a bit more detail.

9 | Bank Reform

We could set up the Common Cashflow Fund under our current banking system but if we did we would be failing to meet the fifth requirement on our list: a stable economic environment that can cope with the forces of creative destruction and natural disaster. Our banks are private businesses which are run by men and women who are driven by the desire to get rich. These people have been responsible for a great deal of creative destruction in the past and there's no reason to assume that they will change their ways. Indeed, some would argue that the creativity of bankers in managing how money is used enables productive economic activity and should therefore be encouraged. The problem with banking as we know it isn't the enthusiasm of bankers to chase profits, it's the framework in which they are allowed to operate.

The most significant problem with the current banking system is the effect that bank lending has on the money supply of the economy. When banks go on a lending spree the amount of money flowing through the economy increases, which first causes inflation in the areas of the economy that are the focus of the lending (e.g. housing) and then a more general inflation as money leaks into the rest of the economy. These inflationary spikes are inevitably followed by a slide into recession as the chosen market gets saturated and the borrowed money is repaid, but the prices that have risen during the boom rarely drop to their previous levels. So we end up with lots of people on reduced incomes struggling with higher prices, unable to make ends meet. The Common Cashflow Fund can easily be increased to take account of the inflationary effect of a bank lending spree, giving everyone enough money every month to cover the increase in household bills. This might stop people from grumbling for a while but it won't help the economy to pull itself out of recession. In fact, it will tend to hold the economy down. If the money supply is shrinking, the CCF payback rate has to increase in order to gather the same amount of money every month to replenish the CCF pot. If the CCF is expanding to take account of inflation at the same time as the money supply is shrinking then the problem is compounded: the payback rate has to increase even further. An increase in the CCF payback rate means that a bigger proportion of the money in the economy is being cycled round and round to pay for the basics, which means there is less money available for investment in the productive economy, which reduces the opportunities for productive people to lift the economy out of recession. Boom and bust is the result of allowing banks to determine the amount of money in the economy. The CCF will help to soften the hardships of the bust but it won't cure the problem. Banking reform is the only answer.

The banking reforms that are proposed by Positive Money are designed to remove the link between bank lending and the amount of money in the economy. Banks make profits from lending money and will therefore lend wherever and whenever there are profits to be made. The fact that banks add new money to the economy whenever they make a loan is a side-effect of the business of banking. That the two things are linked – bank lending and money creation – is an accident of history that no-one has ever bothered to tidy up. Banks are perfectly able to make profits from investing money that's already in the economy, there's no need for them to create new money when they create a loan. Controlling the amount of money in the economy is better done by people whose remit is to keep the economy stable for the benefit of everyone rather than people whose remit is to capture as much money as possible for themselves and their shareholders.

Positive Money proposes decoupling money creation from bank lending by changing the rules of banking so that banks are no longer allowed to create deposits (the money in your bank account) and are only allowed to make loans using money that already exists. To understand the implications of this we have to contradict my earlier assertion that all money is essentially the same and recognise the difference between commercial bank money and central bank money. As we've seen, when you take out a loan the bank simply writes the amount of the loan into your bank account – creating the money out of thin air. In accounting terms this new money in your account isn't money, it's a liability on the bank to pay you that amount of money whenever you demand it. In exchange you give the bank a promise that you'll repay the money, plus interest, over a period of time. In accounting terms this promise is an asset of the bank that balances the liability of the deposit it has created in your account. So, even though you can spend the deposit that the bank has created, in accounting terms what the bank has created isn't money, it's merely a liability. When you use the loan to buy a car, for example, you transfer the deposit from your account to the account of the seller of the car. Let's say that you bank with RBS and the seller banks with HSBC. When your bank (RBS) 'transfers the money' to the seller's account at HSBC what actually happens is that RBS transfers the liability to HSBC. So RBS no longer owes you any money but HSBC now owes money to the seller of the car. On the same day it's likely that HSBC will be transferring liabilities to RBS as people with HSBC accounts buy things from people with RBS accounts. Many of these transfers will cancel each other out over the course of the business day leaving a small balance in favour of one bank or the other. Let's say that, at the end of the day, RBS owes HSBC £10M (a small amount of money for a big bank). This debt is cleared by RBS transferring £10M from its reserve account at the Bank of England to HSBC's reserve account at the Bank of England. This £10M, the money that banks hold in their reserves at the central bank, is regarded by economists as 'real' money. Notes and coins are also regarded as 'real' money because they are created by the Bank of England and the Treasury.

Positive Money proposes turning all money into 'real' money, which can be achieved by converting all of the deposits in commercial banks into money at the Bank of England, removing the distinction between bank deposits and central bank reserves. Your bank will no longer owe you the money that shows up in your bank statement. Instead you will own the money in your account and your bank will merely administer it on your behalf. When the switch to 100% 'real' money occurs everything that the banks currently owe to their customers will instead be owed to the Bank of England. Which means the commercial banks will be massively in debt to the Bank of England, but the debt will be paid down over time using money that the banks get from repayment of loans that were issued before the switch. Instead of disappearing into thin air as it currently does, the principal of these loan repayments will cancel out the liability that the banks took on when their customers deposits were transferred to the Bank of England. This means that the total amount of money in the system will not change as debt is paid off, which means that new money does not have to be created in order to keep the economy working. The result is a constant amount of money available for economic activity instead of the periodic lurch from feast to famine that we get under the current system. The chances of maintaining a stable economy are far greater if the money supply remains stable.

Stability will be further enhanced by Positive Money's proposals for separating the functions of exchange and investment. Under our current system all of the money in your bank accounts belongs to the bank: your account merely shows you how much money the bank owes you. This means that if a bank goes bust all of the money that everyone has in the bank can be lost. At the moment the UK government guarantees to repay up to £85,000 per individual account holder if a bank goes bust, which could be a significant burden on the Treasury (and the taxpayer) if a big bank was to go under. Positive Money proposes that banks offer two distinct types of account: transaction accounts and investment accounts. As outlined earlier, transaction accounts will be like the current accounts that we typically use for managing our everyday spending except that the money in them will belong to us and the bank will not be able to lend or invest any of the money that's held in them. The money will actually be held in the Bank of England and our high street bank will merely be providing us with a system for making and receiving payments. This means that if the bank goes bust our money is safe and all we have to do is transfer the administration of it to a different bank. It also means that the government no longer has to pay compensation if a bank fails. If we decide that we want to get a return from our spare money we'll have to transfer it from our transaction account to an investment account. When we do this we'll be handing our money over to the bank to invest on our behalf. In exchange the bank will give us a promise to repay the money we've invested at some time in the future as well as giving us some of the profits that the bank gets from the investment. It's likely that the banks will offer a range of investment accounts with differing levels of risk and reward. For example, a high risk high reward account might concentrate on investment in the global mining sector and you may have to commit your money to a 5 year term and accept that the income on the investment is paid annually. Conversely, a low risk account that invests in mortgage lending to A-rated borrowers is likely to offer much more modest rewards, perhaps paid on a monthly basis, and a much shorter notice period to withdraw your money. Some investment accounts might concentrate on capital growth rather than providing an income stream for the investor. Others may simply offer a temporary haven from the CCF payback system, offering no additional rewards. For example, a bank might fund overdrafts for some customers by taking short term investments from other customers, effectively balancing transaction accounts that are periodically short of money against those that are typically in surplus. Whatever the banks decide to do with the money in our investment accounts they will have to work hard to reassure us that the risks are worth the rewards on offer because if the investment turns sour or the bank goes bust all of the money that we have invested may be lost and the government won't give us any compensation.

Positive Money's reforms – removing the link between bank lending and money creation, and separating transaction banking from investment banking will help to create a stable platform for our economy but they won't of themselves, cure the dysfunction of our economic system or contribute to the other four things that we need our economy to do for us. There is nothing in Positive Money's proposals that will encourage productive people to be productive. The tax and benefit system will remain as idiotic as it is today, discouraging employers, employees and the unemployed from using their energy and enthusiasm to do useful things. Nor is there anything in the proposals that will help to provide a baseline prosperity for everyone regardless of their circumstances. We'll continue to suffer from a system that struggles to provide the necessities of life to those in need while breeding resentment amongst those who pay for it and dependency amongst those who rely on it. Positive Money's reforms won't do anything to promote a reliable flow of money throughout the economy. People and businesses that have lots of money will continue to hoard it and spend it selectively in particular areas of the economy. The bits of the economy that aren't favoured by the people with the cash will continue to suffer from a lack of liquidity. Positive Money's proposals will have no positive effect on any of the foregoing points but they could have a distinctly negative effect on the fourth of our requirements for a thriving economy: encouraging investment in productive activities.

For a start, there's nothing in the proposals to discourage bankers from using our money as gambling chips. Banking innovation of the last thirty years has meant that banks are very inclined to 'invest' in what they call 'financial assets'. What they're actually doing is gambling. They use money to place bets on changes in the values of other chunks of money (or promises of payment) that are bundled up in a bewildering variety of guises. Speculation in financial assets can be very lucrative for the banks but it damages the rest of the economy because it diverts money away from productive businesses. Worse still, gambling on financial assets can lead to economic disaster. The crash of 2007/08 was triggered by banks having packaged up bundles of debt and sold them back and forward until nobody knew what risks were attached to each so-called asset. This lack of clarity about risk led to a lack of trust between the banks so they stopped lending to each other. Interbank lending is a vital element of our current banking system. If banks don't lend to each other to balance up the differences in loans and deposits then it's highly probable that one or more banks will be unable to balance their books and will go bust. This is what happened in 2007/08 and the fall-out from this pass-the-parcel of toxic assets continues to threaten the health of banks and the well-being of nations in 2013, with no end to the crisis in sight. Allowing banks to use our money to gamble on financial assets provides few benefits for the productive economy but lots of opportunities for economic chaos. Gambling with our money can be much more lucrative for bankers than investing it in productive activities because the risks are perceived to be easier to calculate and the performance of a few traders handling billions of pounds is supposed to be easier to monitor than the performance of a million businesses each of which has borrowed a few thousand pounds. Positive Money's reforms mean that bankers will no longer have an unlimited amount of money from which to make profits. There will be a finite amount of money in the economy and a significant proportion of it will be held in transaction accounts, unavailable for investment, so bankers won't be able to make any profit from it. In these circumstances bankers could be inclined to use the majority of the limited money available to them for gambling, which will leave the productive economy short of investment.

To make matters worse, there's a definite risk that people will choose to keep most of their money safely in transaction accounts regardless of the fact it's not earning interest. Allowing bankers to invest our money without the safety net of a government bailout if the investment goes wrong involves a leap of faith. The banking crisis of 2007/08 seriously damaged the reputation of bankers as reliable custodians of our money but they show few signs of acknowledging the harm that they have done to the economy. This indifference is due to the fact that very little has changed in the way that banks do business. They still have almost absolute power over the money in our economy and bankers still use this power primarily for the benefit of themselves and their shareholders. We are more or less forced to give them the money that we have and they can do more or less what they like with it. We are obliged to borrow from them the money that we need to make the economy work, and they have significant power over what we can spend it on. The effect of their allocation of money on the economy is a secondary consideration: their primary focus is profit. In 2012, four years after the financial crisis of 2007/08 hit us, the UK is still bumping along on the brink of recession with no end in sight. Individuals and small businesses struggle to find the money that they need to keep themselves solvent yet the banks refuse to invest in these parts of the economy that need it most. Instead they concentrate on lucrative gambling activities and continue to pay themselves huge salaries and bonuses. We see bankers as greedy and dishonest so why would we trust them with our money when we will be able to keep it nice and safe in a transaction account? Idle money tucked away in our transaction accounts is safe money. Active money, at the mercy of the bankers, is at risk. Under the reformed banking system, as proposed by Positive Money, there will be a strong incentive to play safe, which will starve the productive economy of the investment that it needs in order to thrive. Those of us who are willing to risk investing some of our money are likely to be very cautious where we put it because of our distrust of bankers and the absence of a government safety net. Of the limited supply of money available for investment accounts there could be a tendency for the bulk of it to be concentrated in sectors that are considered safe and reliable. This could make life difficult for people who are trying to innovate, and for small businesses that are often seen to be higher risk. A lack of money flowing from banks to a wide range of commercial enterprises will depress activity across the productive economy, which will reduce the availability and quality of the goods and services we need to make our lives comfortable and enjoyable. On their own, there is a serious danger of Positive Money's reforms crippling the economy by discouraging investment in productive activities, but the CCF payback system will act as an antidote to this tendency. The payback system will be a deterrent to gambling on financial assets because all of the money that's being used, and any profits that are captured on the deals, will be liable for CCF payback at a rate of 0.0034% per hour, which is equivalent to 0.81% per day, or 2.46%

per month, or 25.5% per annum. This is a significant overhead for the gamblers. Using money to 'make money' will no longer be such an attractive option, which will reduce the risk of a banking crisis that's triggered by speculating on dodgy financial assets. The payback system will also put pressure on money that's lying idle in transaction accounts. People will be more inclined to risk investing some of their spare money to make up for what's being shaved off into the CCF pot.

Another concern with Positive Money's reforms is their plan for how new money is created and distributed. Positive Money proposes that the Bank of England will create new money periodically on instruction from the Money Creation Committee (MCC), which will replace the current body that's responsible for trying to control the money supply, The Monetary Policy Committee (MPC). Independent from government, the MPC tries to keep inflation at a suitable level by adjusting interest rates and influencing the money supply through buying and selling government bonds. Even in the best of times no-one could be certain that these tools were effective but recent years have proved that they are of limited use. Being able to control absolutely the creation of new money will give the Money Creation Committee a much better chance of keeping the money supply at levels that are appropriate for the whole economy, not just those bits that the banks favour. However, deciding how much money the economy needs in order to thrive is always going to be an inexact science and there will be times that the MCC gets it wrong, resulting in some degree of economic stagnation or turmoil. Positive Money's proposals offer nothing to mitigate the effects of these errors by the MCC. Under the CCF system a key part of the MCC's responsibility will be to develop a formula that gives a realistic value for the cost of living, which can be used to calculate the CCF monthly shares for adults and children. As the economy trundles onwards through good times and bad, this formula will tell us if the monthly CCF share is enough to meet our basic needs, and trigger an automatic adjustment of the CCF as required. This mechanism will ensure that everyone has enough money to live off regardless of what is happening elsewhere in the economy. Giving the responsibility for the CCF calculation to the MCC (an independent body that is answerable to parliament as a whole, rather than the government) will ensure that the individuals on the committee are always aware of the prime importance of the personal economies of individual citizens. Instead of adjusting something as esoteric as interest rates or aggregate money supply in the hope that they will have some positive effect on household budgets the MCC will have direct control over the minimum amount of money that everyone needs in order to survive.

Another troubling aspect of Positive Money's proposals is that any new money that's sanctioned by the MCC and created by the Bank of England should be given to the government. They suggest that allowing the government to decide how new money should be spent is the most democratic way to inject new money into the economy. Many people would question the wisdom of this.

Without a doubt the money will be spent wherever it will do most good for the government, which is not the same thing as doing most good for the economy as a whole. The money will be directed to areas of the economy that are of particular interest to government ministers or professional lobbyists who are able to influence government decisions. Furthermore, if distribution of the money is being administered by the government a considerable proportion of it will get absorbed by government employees and suppliers, concentrating the effects of the new money in a small and privileged area of the economy. There's almost no chance that the economy as a whole will benefit from any new money that's given to the government, so Positive Money's suggestion is certainly not the most democratic solution. The CCF system, in contrast, provides a means of distributing new money through the economy in a much more diffuse and democratic way. When the MCC instructs the Bank of England to create new money it can be divided equally among the entire population of the UK and distributed as a bonus along with our CCF monthly share. This removes any chance of government lobbying the Bank of England for new money for a particular purpose, and removes any chance of special interest groups lobbying government to spend the new money in a particular way. Spreading new money through the economy by giving everyone an equal share of it will contribute to all five of our requirements for a thriving economy.

10 | Workforce

Some people will be horrified at the proposal to give every adult £1,000/month for ***doing nothing***. Surely this is a licence for people to stay in their beds instead of getting up to do an honest day's work. If you take away the fear of poverty what incentive will there be to for anyone to do anything, especially all the dirty, hard, and tedious jobs? No-one will sweep the streets or empty the bins and the country will go to hell in a handcart. This point of view, however, assumes that money is the only motivation for going to work, but our relationship with paid employment is a lot more complex. Around half of the population of the UK gets the money that it needs in exchange for doing some sort of work, but the importance of paid work extends beyond the need for a weekly wage. Our culture places a social value on being in employment. In many ways our work defines us within our communities, giving us a recognisable position in the social matrix. Generally, someone who has a job is given more respect than someone who doesn't, regardless of the type of work that's being done. Indeed for many people the fact of 'having' a job is of greater importance to them than the work that they actually do. Being part of a team of people and being useful to that team are things that many people value very highly and miss terribly if they are made redundant or forced into retirement. The Common Cashflow Fund won't alter these cultural attitudes to employment but it will have other significant effects on relationships between employers and employees.

There has always been an imbalance of power between employers and their employees. In the days before welfare benefits, if you didn't have a job or any other source of income, or any money put by, you were in serious trouble. Without money to buy food or pay rent you would soon find yourself homeless and hungry. The patronage of an employer paying a living wage was, for many, the difference between life and death, and that gave business owners a tremendous amount of power over their workers. Even now, the fear of being cast out of a job and left to the not-so-tender care of the welfare state means that employees are wary of how they deal with the people who hire and fire. This imbalance is recognised in employment legislation, which has almost entirely been enacted to protect employees from employers and not the other way around. The Common Cashflow Fund will, to a large extent, dissipate this power that bosses have over workers. The universal right to a guaranteed annual income of £12,000 for an individual or £24,000 for a couple will remove much of the fear of unemployment, giving people more space in which to make choices about how and when they sell their labour. Employees will be less inclined to accept poor working conditions, being taken for granted, or being bullied by unpleasant bosses. Why would you stick around to be abused when you know there will be enough money coming in every month to pay the rent and the grocery bills? As the threat of unemployment becomes less potent the relationship between employers and employees will become more balanced and it's likely that the ways in which work is done will change. The traditional full-time, long term contract is likely to be replaced in many cases by a more flexible relationship where employment becomes focused on the execution of tasks rather than the occupation of a position. We will be more inclined to talk about "doing" a job than "having" as job, and contracts of employment will change accordingly. More people will behave like self-employed contractors, negotiating with businesses to take on specific projects or to fulfil a role at times that suit both parties. Hopefully this change in the power balance between employer and employee will render much of current employment legislation redundant. If employees no longer fear unemployment (thanks to the CCF) then they no longer need the protection of legislation, much of which can be abused by lazy or incompetent workers, their union reps and their lawyers. With the fear of unemployment eliminated by the CCF, employer and employee should be free to trade on their reputations. A bad employer will struggle to get good staff in the same way that a bad employee will struggle to find work. Unless they mend their ways the former will surely go out of business while the latter will be stuck with the basic standard of living provided by the CCF.

Fears that the Common Cashflow Fund will reduce us to a country of layabouts don't stack up. The CCF will only give us enough money to pay for the basics that we need to survive – food, housing, clothing, and local travel costs. Some people will be content with this but a great many others will not. Having spare money to spend gives us choice over what we eat, how we dress, where we live, how we travel, and what we do to entertain ourselves, and these choices are open to us only if we have enough money to spend. For most of us the only way to get enough money to make these choices is to work for it. The CCF won't give us enough money to make the most of the choices on offer so we will continue to go to work and do useful things for each other so that we get enough spare money to spend on stuff that we desire. As well as giving us more money to spend, going to work protects us from the tyranny of boredom. Although many of us complain about being run off our feet and enjoy a few days of rest and recreation very few of us are comfortable with a life of idleness. We are sociable creatures who thrive on communal activity: we like to be wanted, we enjoy doing things for each other, and much of that need to be useful is satisfied by going to work, none of which will change when the CCF is providing us with £1,000/month. What may change is the number of hours that people are prepared to work each week and the amount of money that people will be prepared to accept in return for the work that they do. I have never understood why we expect to pay a plumber £30/hour to replace a broken toilet seat but a cleaner only gets £6/hour to clean the toilet. Both jobs are equally valuable to the user of the toilet and both can be done by a willing novice after a few minutes of training. Cleaners are offered low wages because of economic geography - everyone knows that the minimum wage is the going rate for a cleaner so that's what they are given. Cleaners accept low wages because they need the money in order to live. There may be some cleaners who love their work and will be happy to continue doing what they do for low wages even when they're getting £1,000/month from the CCF, but I suspect most people who do hard, unpleasant or boring jobs will be unlikely to work for a few pounds an hour after the CCF system kicks in. If we want people to clean our toilets, wash our dishes, polish our floors, and do all of the other so-called menial tasks that we currently take for granted, we're probably going to have to offer them something more attractive than the minimum wage. The CCF will change the way that we value different types of work, especially those that are hard and unpleasant, because there will no longer be a supply of workers who are desperate for a job. Employers will probably find that the cost of tasks like cleaning will rise significantly but this will be balanced out by lower taxes (as discussed earlier) and a reduction in the costs of other tasks. Book-keeping, for example, will become much simpler if we abolish national insurance and get rid of VAT, allowing book-keepers to work fewer hours or use their spare time to do something more productive than collect tax for the government. And although the wage bill for cleaners will probably rise there are some cases where the CCF might encourage people to work for less money. As part of the legislation that brings the CCF system into being it would be wise to abolish the minimum wage and allow employers to reduce the wages and salaries of employees by a maximum of £1,000/month. Some people who are relatively well paid might accept the full reduction of £1,000/month because they enjoy their work, are ambitious to further their career, and their total income would remain unchanged. At the lower end of the scale, someone who's currently paid £1,100/month is very unlikely to turn up for work if his salary is reduced to £100. Many middle income workers may accept a reduction in their hourly rate while others may negotiate a higher rate but be happy to work fewer hours each week. This will give employers the opportunity to more closely match the effort and skills of their employees with the work that needs to be done. Instead of paying someone a full-time salary for work that is intermittent an employer will be able to pay to get work done as and when it is required. This is a much more efficient use of labour, resulting in lower costs for employers and more freedom for employees. As well as adjusting their working hours to suit an employer many people may choose to reduce their working time even further, which will create lots of part-time opportunities for other people who are currently keen but unable to get work in a particular field. So, even if we give employers the right to reduce salaries by £1,000/month it's unlikely that many employees will accept this much of a reduction in what they're being paid. Whatever the results of negotiations over remuneration it's highly likely that the CCF will stabilise wages and salaries. The fact that the CCF monthly shares are linked to the cost of living means that their value will be maintained, which will suppress demands for wage increases. Stable wage bills make it easier for businesses to make investment decisions and to remain competitive in domestic and international markets, all of which is good for the economy.

Unemployment amongst young people is currently a serious problem throughout the UK and beyond. In December 2012 the government reported that unemployment among 16 – 24 year olds in the UK was more than 20% and in other parts of Europe the figure is even higher. In a depressed economy jobs are scarce and any that do become available tend to be filled by experienced workers who have come from businesses that have closed down. This means that opportunities for young, inexperienced workers are thin on the ground. Even when an economy is vibrant the costs associated with employing young people are unattractive because it takes time and money to turn a novice into a productive employee. In some industries young people are offered unpaid internships where they get to learn about the job while the employer gets to see what they're capable of. If all goes well the internship can lead to a proper job. This system can work very well for both parties but only if the intern has some way of supporting themselves while they are working for no pay, which generally means that only the offspring of rich parents can afford to become interns. Under the CCF system every adult will have an income of £1,000/month which means that everyone will be able to support themselves through an internship. The pool of candidates for internships will expand dramatically, which will allow a much broader range of businesses to adopt the internship model offering lots of young people lots of opportunities to get a foothold on the career ladder of their choosing. The CCF will also make it much easier for young people to spend time in college and university as they will no longer have to borrow money to cover their living expenses. By creating the environment in which young people can learn without having to earn money the CCF will help to provide our economy with a continuously productive workforce rather than leaving the younger generation drifting about wondering when they are going to be able to make a start in the world of work.

Fear that the CCF will turn us into a bunch of layabouts is even more irrational when we consider how many of us currently work for no financial reward whatsoever. There are probably more than 2 million stay-at-home parents in the UK who spend their time housekeeping and looking after children, relying on their partner or welfare benefits for income. These people work every bit as hard as those of us who are in paid employment and they will continue to do so under the CCF system, but life will be a whole lot easier from them thanks to the guaranteed monthly income for themselves and their children. There are also an estimated 6.4 million people in the UK who provide unpaid full-time or part-time care to relatives and friends who are chronically ill or disabled. Again, most of these people currently get the money that they need to survive from a family member who's in employment or from welfare benefits. They will continue to do this work but the CCF will transform their lives as they will have the benefit of their own monthly share as well as that of the person that they're looking after. In addition to parents and carers the other significant group of people who work without being paid any money for their efforts are volunteers. A Citizenship Survey in 2011 estimated that more than 19 million people in the UK undertook work on a voluntary basis at least once a year, with around 15 million of these volunteering at least once a month. Those of us who do voluntary work are obviously motivated by something other than financial reward and will continue to volunteer under the CCF system. Indeed, it's likely that the guaranteed income from the CCF will encourage more people to spend some of their time doing useful work on a voluntary basis.

So, while it is likely that the Common Cashflow Fund will change the relationship between employers and employees, alter our patterns of working, and shift the economic geography so that dirty and difficult jobs are properly remunerated there is little to suggest that it will stop us from being productive or taking care of each other. It should also make the business of government a whole lot easier.

11 | Government

Governing a nation has always seemed to me to be a thankless task. On the one hand the population clamours for better services, which invariably cost more money to provide, while on the other hand the people complain about high taxes and do everything in their power to avoid paying. The unfortunate souls who have been elected to make decisions on taxation and spending, along with the civil servants who have to turn these policy decisions into services and systems that actually work, have chosen a very hard row to hoe. Mind you, politicians are guilty of creating a rod for their own backs by pretending that they have much more control over the health of the economy than is actually the case. This pretence gives government ministers a sense of their own importance but it also means that they are blamed for all of the ills that are visited on their citizens as a result of economic sclerosis. In reality, the appetite of the banks to lend money is what drives (or hinders) an economy, and recent years have shown that governments have very little power over the lending policies of commercial banks. A government can do no more than react to whatever the economic climate throws at us, and it invariably finds itself short of umbrellas and raincoats just when they are most needed. The reforms proposed by Positive Money and the Common Cashflow Fund will not give the government any more control over the economic weather but they will reduce the volatility of the climate and relieve ministers of a substantial burden of responsibility.

The banking reforms that are proposed by Positive Money will provide the economy with a stable money supply which will go a long way to removing the boom and bust cycles that have bedevilled us for so long. Without the temptations of the boom and the restrictions of the bust to deal with, governments will spend less time fire-fighting and have more chance of developing and implementing policies that make our collective lives better in the long term. Banking reform will stabilise the foundations of our economy, making the job of government much easier, but the most dramatic changes to the business of government will come as a result of the Common Cashflow Fund. The CCF will eliminate the need for almost every kind of benefit that is currently dished out in order to help people meet their day to day living costs. In 2010 the Institute for Fiscal Studies (IFS) calculated that the UK government paid the following amounts in benefits: £34,115M to families with children; £4,853M to the unemployed; £41,584M to people who are in work but don't earn enough to make ends meet; £78,411M to the elderly; £28,565M to people who are too ill or disabled to earn a living; and £685M to people who faced hardship after the death of a family member. That was a total of £188,213M of expenditure on benefits to help people cover their basic living costs, all of which had to be paid out by the government in 2010, and then collected via taxes so that it could be paid out again in 2011, and so on. The vast majority of the money that the government pays out in benefits is spent into the economy within a month or two, where it becomes exposed to the taxation system, so it could be argued that the same money is collected as taxes and distributed as benefits over and over on an annual cycle. There would be no problem with this system if the amount of money collected in taxes each year by the government was equal to or greater than the amount that it spends, but this is not the case. As well as dishing out c.£190,000M on welfare benefits each year the government spends hundreds of thousands of millions of pounds on education, health, defence, transport, and lots of other stuff that we expect our public services to take care of on our behalf, and there is never enough revenue from taxation to meet all of these expenses. The tax sum is always less than the spend sum, and the only way to close the gap is to borrow. In 2012 the government borrowed c.£120,000M so that it had enough money to cover its spending commitments, and this was a government that had been elected on the promise of reducing borrowing and had made substantial cuts in public services in order to try to meet this election pledge. It is blindingly obvious that our current tax-and-spend system doesn't work: it is in fact a tax-and-borrow-and-spend system where the burden of borrowing becomes heavier every year thanks to the interest payments on the accumulated debt. At the end of 2012 the total UK government debt was estimated to be c.£1,350,000M on which we had to make annual interest payments totalling c.£46,000M. If the government has to borrow the same in 2013 as it did in 2012, by the end of the year the total debt will have risen to c.£1,471,000M, which is likely to cost us c.£50,000M in interest payments. This is clearly unsustainable but I can find no evidence of a plausible strategy or plan to get us out of this spiral of debt. Deficit hawks in many countries talk boldly of slashing the size of government in order to get government borrowing under control but the cuts in public services that would be required would never be accepted by the electorates, so, short of bloody revolution, they will never happen. Could the Common Cashflow Fund provide government with the means to escape from the black hole of debt into which it is being inexorably drawn? Possibly.

By converting our notes and coins into CCF money and recycling it every month through the payback system we will eliminate c.£190,000M of annual government spending on welfare benefits. In addition to handing out money in the form of benefits the government currently supports people who have limited incomes by giving them a variety of tax credits and allowances. These effectively allow people to keep an extra chunk of their income that would otherwise be collected by the taxman and added to the government's coffers. For example everyone gets a personal tax allowance which means that the first few thousand pounds of income (e.g. £8,105 in 2012-13 for those under the age of 65) is tax free. The CCF monthly share, which will be untaxed, will be a direct replacement for this allowance. The value of these tax credits and allowances in 2010-11, according to HMRC, was c.£85,000M. Under the CCF system none of these allowances will be required because everyone will have enough income to meet their daily needs, so the government will be able to collect this money via the taxation system. Changes to the taxation system post CCF may change the value of these allowances but if we add their current value to the total benefits bill we find that the government will be c.£275,000M better off each year thanks to the CCF. According to Treasury statistics the total expenditure of the UK government in 2010-11 was £691,666M, so the CCF could reduce government spending by as much as 40%. I say "could" because there will be many people who would like maintain the current taxation regime alongside the CCF and use the spare money to fund all sorts of government programmes, such as social housing, energy efficiency, or new warships. This would be a mistake. Although people with lots of spare money will certainly work out strategies to minimise the amount of money they lose to the CCF payback system, there will be many productive businesses that have to hold large amounts of money in their bank accounts at all times. For these businesses CCF payback will feel exactly like a tax. If we maintain the current tax regime the CCF payback system will effectively be an additional tax on this type of business. As discussed earlier a taxation system that penalises work and commerce is counter-productive, discouraging the very activities that provide us with all of the things that we need to make our lives secure and comfortable. By reducing government spending by c.40% the CCF gives us the opportunity to get rid of some of the stupidest taxes that currently add to the cost of exchanging goods and services and discourage productive people from being productive.

VAT (sales tax) is universally unpopular. Consumers hate it because it inflates the price of almost everything that they buy and businesses hate it because they have the administrative chore of collecting it on behalf of the government. It's also a direct tax on commerce, and commerce is what provides us with all of the things that we need in order to live in safety and comfort. Abolishing VAT will act as a major stimulus to the economy by lowering prices, reducing the cost of doing business, and it will go some way to compensating businesses for the money that they will lose to the CCF payback system. National Insurance Contributions (NICs) are taxes paid by employees and employers, which are recorded against the name of the individual employee. If that individual is in need of government assistance at some future date the value of these contributions is used to calculate the amount of money that they are given as welfare benefits. Despite the nominal link between an individual employee and their future needs NICs are really just part of the mainstream tax system: the money gets put into the Treasury pot and used for general government spending. Although the intentions behind the original National Insurance scheme were laudable, NICs are a tax on employment and, as such, discourage businesses from taking on more staff, which inhibits the commercial economy. These negative effects of NICs make them prime candidates for abolition, and when we realise that the CCF is a direct replacement for all of the benefits that are nominally paid for by NICs the case for abolition is unassailable, if we can afford it. We've seen how the Common Cashflow Fund will reduce government spending by c.£275,000M each year. In 2011-12 government revenue from National Insurance Contributions was c.£100,000M, so if we abolish NICs we'll still have c.£175,000M to play with. Her Majesty's Revenue & Customs collected c.£100,000M of sales tax in 2011-12, so if we abolish VAT as well as NICs we're still left with a surplus of c.£75,000M. There will be lots of people with lots of good ideas for making use of £75,000M every year but in the early years of the CCF my vote would go to using this surplus to stop the spiral of government debt. Imagine how popular the Chancellor of the Exchequer would be if she announced that the annual deficit would be reduced from c.£120,000M to c.£45,000M without any cuts in public services. And it gets even better. The new deficit of c.£45,000M is conveniently very similar to the annual interest payments on the accumulated government debt. If the government was able to exchange its current debts, which bear interest, for loans that were interest free then there would be no £46,000M of interest to pay so deficit would disappear.

Governments borrow when they don't have enough money on hand to pay for immediate expenses. Essentially they have cashflow problems which they currently fix by borrowing money that they agree to repay on a certain date along with a chunk of extra money, the interest on the loan. The people who lend to the government are in the driving seat: they can choose whether or not to lend depending on the interest rate on offer and what alternative investment opportunities are available. The CCF payback system, however, shifts the balance of power away from those who have money lying idle towards those who are ready to put money to work. Under the CCF payback system idle money is being eroded at a rate of more than 2% each month so people who have money to spare will be very keen to lend it to someone else in order to protect its value. When the government is short of cash to meet its short term spending needs it will certainly be able to borrow from commercial banks at zero interest, and may even be able to get some loans at negative interest, meaning that the government would end up paying back less money to the lender than it had borrowed. Imagine a bank that has been very successful with its investments and has money coming in faster than it can find new projects in which to invest. Say the bank has £100M of spare money sloshing about but it will be a month or so before it has any use for it. Every hour 0.0034% of the £100M is being siphoned off into the Common Cashflow Fund at the Bank of England, which adds up to a loss of more than £2M per month. The government, meanwhile, is waiting for a periodic chunk of tax revenue and finds itself a bit short of funds, so it offers to take the £100M off the bank's hands for 30 days, at the end of which period the government will repay the bank £99M. Instead of losing £2M to the CCF payback system the bank will only lose £1M and the government has had the use of £100M of money at a cost of only £99M. For longer term borrowing government bonds might be sold to investors at 0% interest, providing the government with interest-free funding for capital projects. In return the investors are given a haven for their money, safe from the CCF payback system. Over time, all of the government's £1,350,000M of debt could be converted into loans at zero or negative interest, which would wipe out the current annual interest payments of £46,000M, which would reduce the annual deficit to zero.

Another benefit of the CCF would be a significant reduction in the size of government. Our current system of recycling money via taxation and benefits is hugely complicated, requiring armies of civil servants to interpret and administer the rules that politicians dream up. Most of this gargantuan effort is applied to minimising misery rather than adding to the sum of human happiness. A government officer who spends his life moving bits of information around in the Department of Work and Pensions could make himself and others much happier by using his time to create or grow or produce something that gives people sustenance or pleasure. Government departments are full of human potential that is largely wasted on tedious administrative tasks, many of which will be eliminated by the CCF. We should take the opportunity to release these people from the bondage of bureaucracy and let them use their talents to do things that add to our quality of life. The CCF will present the government with many other opportunities to reduce spending. For instance, there are some individuals whose upkeep becomes the responsibility of the state, the costs of which are currently borne by the government. Prisoners, orphans, people who need long term care in secure hospitals are examples that spring to mind where the CCF monthly shares can be automatically transferred from these individuals to the organisations that are looking after them, relieving government of a significant proportion of the costs of such care. It's also possible that government will see savings from a reduction in crime. When everyone gets a regular income from the CCF there will be less of an incentive for people to steal the things that they need or desire. Thieves will find it much more difficult to steal money if we stop using coins and notes and replace them with electronic cash. It will be still be possible to steal the cards and phones that are used to make payments but, as is now the case, getting past the security features that are built into these is infinitely more difficult than stealing and spending banknotes. As these crimes of theft and robbery disappear so do the costs of detection and conviction.

The CCF will also get rid of a major headache for government – the pensions time bomb. Actuaries (the people who calculate how many pensioners we're likely to have in the future and how much money we will need to support them) have been telling us for years that the present systems of pension provision are wholly inadequate because of our increased life expectancy. If we keep going as we are we will soon reach a point where the government's tax revenues will not be able to pay for even the most basic of state pensions for all of the people in the country who are too old and infirm to work for a living, nor will the government be able to afford to compensate people who have been conned into buying worthless pensions from the private sector. This has been called the pensions time bomb and when it explodes the majority of the population will find that poverty is a constant companion in old age. The CCF will defuse this time bomb, giving everyone enough money to live in security and comfort regardless of how unlucky they have been with their attempts to build up a nest egg for their retirement.

The Common Cashflow Fund means that the government will no longer have to find money to pay welfare benefits but there will still be plenty for the politicians and bureaucrats to do to. The CCF does no more than provide an economic backstop for the population, and the payback system merely encourages us to make productive use of money. As is now the case, our prosperity will rest on the efforts of the people who drive the productive economy, doing and making stuff that contributes to our comfort and security. Government has a huge influence over the climate in which these productive people operate and must adapt itself to the changes that the CCF will bring to ensure that it is easy for productive people to get things done. For me, the biggest changes that government will have to make are in taxation, regulation, and education.

If we assume that the advent of the Common Cashflow Fund is accompanied by the demise of National Insurance Contributions and VAT then we will be left with only two main taxes that penalise productive people: income tax and corporation tax. After the CCF is up and running, I would argue strongly that the government should look for alternative ways of raising revenues that currently come from taxing the earnings of individuals and businesses. Taxing the production of carbon dioxide, for example, would tend to reduce the rate at which we gobble up the world's oil, gas, and coal, which would be a good thing for future generations (whether or not you believe in climate change). Carbon taxes have always been resisted partly because they are seen as unfair on the poorer members of society who are disproportionately affected by changes in the cost of oil and gas, and compensating them would be extremely difficult and expensive under our cumbersome benefits system. Under the CCF, however, any rise in living costs as the result of a carbon tax would be reflected in the value of the CCF monthly share which is adjusted to take account of such events. This makes taxing carbon a practical option and gives us the opportunity to abolish income tax and corporation tax. According to the IFS in 2011-12 the Treasury raised around £153,000M from income tax and £42,000M from corporation tax – a total of c.£195,000M. In the same year the Department of Energy & Climate Change (DECC) estimates that the UK produced around 479 million tonnes of carbon dioxide. So, if we decided to abolish income tax and corporation tax and get the same revenue from taxing CO^2 instead the tax on a kg of CO^2 would have to be around 41p. Using figures from The Carbon Trust and the DECC, I reckon that a CO^2 tax of £0.41/kg would increase the cost of domestic energy (gas and electricity) from c.£1,300 to c. £3,300 a year for the average UK household, a jump of around £2,000. A CO^2 tax of 41p/kg will also raise the price of petrol by around 95p, which means the cost of driving an average car for a typical 10,000 miles a year will increase by around £330. All of this sounds horrendous but if someone in this average household is earning at the UK average of £26,500 per annum the abolition of income tax and NICs will mean that they get to keep around £4,000 more of their income than is currently the case. A CO^2 tax at this level will certainly increase the costs of producing and transporting food and household goods but the abolition of VAT will also reduce the prices of many items by as much as 20%, so although the relative costs of things may change the average household budget will probably not see much in the way of losses, and these will be more than compensated for by the guaranteed monthly income from the CCF. As well as replacing taxes that currently punish productive people the carbon tax would give each of us a bit of control over how much tax we pay. If we change our behaviour (e.g. turn off lights when they're not needed and learn how to programme our central heating system) or invest in energy-efficient stuff so that we use less energy our carbon tax bills will go down.

We've already discussed how the government may have to regulate the housing market to ensure that housing costs are not inflated by people who are looking for somewhere to store their wealth, and how this could be done by restricting mortgages to the rebuild value of the property, and restricting rents to a percentage of this same value. There may be other areas of the economy where the government will have to change the ways in which it regulates our behaviour. For example, the CCF payback system will doubtless be the inspiration for a thousand clever schemes for manipulating money, some of which may go against the spirit of the CCF and result in a corruption of the new culture of using money for the good of the economy rather than as a store for wealth. The government will have to be vigilant in this respect and be prepared to legislate to protect us from the worst effects of such schemers and their schemes. In other areas the government may have to act as a facilitator so that our society can adjust to the changes that the CCF will bring. For instance, if the CO^2 tax increases the costs of commuting it may be necessary to adapt planning policies to allow more of a mix of housing, shops and offices in close proximity so that more people are able to walk and cycle to where they need to be instead of having to drive or take the bus. There will also be areas where the government will be able to deregulate, removing legislation that was intended to protect people under the old system but is now redundant. We've already touched on the fact that some employment laws will no longer be required when the fear of unemployment is eliminated, and others will doubtless become apparent as the reforms to the way in which we use money change our everyday lives.

Perhaps the most important change that government can make under the reformed system is in what and how we teach our young people when they are in formal education. It is, of course, essential that everyone leaves school with a thorough understanding of the new system of money and banking so that they are able to make informed decisions about how they manage their money, but of equal importance is a change in the way that our education system prepares our young people for the world of work. We send our children to secondary school around the age of twelve where they spend the next five or six years turning into young adults before being let loose into the world. Our school system is based on a model from the 19th century where scholars sit at desks and are fed information about a range of individual subjects on which they are periodically examined to check whether or not they have listened, understood, and inwardly digested said information. During these years of compulsory education the students learn little or nothing of their importance as the next generation of productive people – the people on whose energy and ingenuity the world will have to rely for the next 30 years. Nor do they learn much about how things are invented, developed, made, grown, processed, organised, distributed, recycled, or given any experience of what it's like to be involved in making any of these things happen. The Common Cashflow Fund will provide every young person with enough money to feed and house themselves after they leave school but it won't give them the vision to see the opportunities and responsibilities that come with adulthood. If we continue to educate our youngsters to merely learn facts and pass exams, and then give them enough money to live off when they leave school, we will be in danger of creating a generation of consumers who will struggle to make the transition into the productive people that our economy needs. Government can help to ensure that this doesn't happen by encouraging our secondary education to change from a fact-gathering exam-passing chore to a time when we learn the science and art of getting things done. School needs to become a place where youngsters learn the habits of collaboration and industriousness, of tackling tasks from conception to completion. They need to discover the satisfaction of doing stuff, of making things happen that are of tangible benefit to themselves and others. Let classrooms become workshops where things are designed and built. Let the cleaning and maintenance of the school buildings be done by the scholars. Let the pupils grow and harvest the fruit and vegetables that are prepared and served-up by their classmates in the school canteen. Let them organise the timetables, attend to the administration, run the IT systems, manage the budgets, write and produce the school plays, run music festivals, look after the library, curate art exhibitions. The hard facts of science, mathematics, English, history, geography, languages, and all of the rest of the curriculum can be taught during these productive activities, putting learning into context, turning information into knowledge. For our economy to thrive we need young people to come out of school bristling with energy and enthusiasm, and equipped with the skills and confidence that they need to go straight into the world of work and be productive.

12 | Our Money

We're told that some of the earliest examples of money can be found in Babylonian culture c.1800BC where lines were scratched on clay blocks to record who owed what to whom. Similar methods of recording credits and debts were employed throughout history and continued to be used in England up until 1826 in the form of tally sticks – pieces of wood with notches carved into them. History suggests, therefore, that money was firmly established as a unit of account long before its value got linked with that of gold and silver. Money in the form of metal coins appears to have arrived later and probably became popular because it made collecting taxes easier for emperors and kings. When money was nothing more than a record of debts and credits arising from trade it's easy to imagine that the stuff being traded – grain, olive oil, timber, spices, cloth, cattle, and the labour needed for harvesting, processing and transporting stuff – would be the focus of people's aspirations. Land, ships, manpower, livestock and goods would be the measure of wealth. But when money takes the form of a precious metal its value becomes tangled up with the scarcity of the metal on which the record of account is inscribed, and ownership of money becomes something to be desired for its own sake. Using precious metal as money means the value of money as a system for exchanging goods becomes confused with the value of money as a possession. The idea of money as a possession to be desired and hoarded has persisted right up until the present day, which means that we take every opportunity to grab and hold as much of it as we possibly can. But money is no longer made of precious metal. Most of it is just numbers in a computer that have no inherent value at all, just like the lumps of clay in Babylonian times, and yet we still want to capture it, have it, hold it until death do us part. This utterly irrational desire to own numbers in a computer would be merely quaint if it didn't adversely affect our economy. But we discovered earlier in the book that hoarding money strangles our economy, starving it of the oxygen that it needs to keep us supplied with all of the stuff that makes our lives comfortable and secure. Every pound that we stash away in our bank accounts to give us an illusion of wealth is a pound that isn't spent, but spending money is what makes our economy work. For our economy to thrive money must be available and mobile – you, me, and everyone else must have access to it. If we are serious about making our economy work properly and eliminating poverty – a shameful disgrace in this world of plenty – we have to drag ourselves out of the Middle Ages and stop pretending that our money is made of gold and silver. We have to recognise that modern money is just numbers in a computer and its value lies solely in our agreement to use it as a medium of exchange. The money in your bank account is nothing more than information. It tells you what your potential spending power is but it has no real value until the moment that you exchange it for something that you need or desire, something that has a real value. If we want our economy to flourish we have to acknowledge the genius of using money as a means of exchange and admit to the sheer stupidity of hoarding lines and dots in a computer as though they were grains of gold and silver. You have to get over the notion that the money in your bank account is your personal possession and replace it with the idea that money is a tool that we own collectively, to be used for our common good. The bit of the tool that's lying in your bank account is merely stored there temporarily until such time as you are ready to use it. We also have to turn on its head the idea that saving is good and spending is bad. Money that's sitting idle in a bank account indefinitely is dead: the tool is left on the shelf turning to rust and nobody is any better off. In contrast, spending money is a win-win scenario: the buyer gets something that she values and the seller gets a turn of using the money tool to buy something that he values, and so the process goes on and on with winners emerging from both sides of every transaction that the money tool makes happen. For those of you who worry about the effect of all of this commerce on the material resources of the planet remember that spending doesn't necessarily mean personal consumption. We can just as easily spend the money on ephemeral entertainment that enriches our souls, or invest it in some collaborative enterprise that will use material resources in an efficient way to increase the wealth and prosperity of large numbers of people. The important thing is that the money keeps moving, allowing productive people to get things done. The key concept for us to grasp is worth repeating: the money in your bank account does not belong to you, nor does the money in my account belong to me. All of it, regardless of where it is in the system, belongs to all of us. It's **our** money: a tool that we own collectively and if we use it wisely, for our common good, it will allow productive people to prosper and ensure that everyone is able to live a life of comfort and security.

The changes that are being proposed in this book may appear to be so revolutionary that it is hard to believe that they can actually happen, but our society is remarkably good at changing, especially when what's on offer will clearly be better than what's gone before. Electricity, telephones, motor vehicles and the road network on which they run, the National Health Service, decimalization of the currency, electronic money, computerisation and the internet: all of these things have been revolutionary – radically changing how we live our lives – and yet we have taken them in our stride. Changing the way in which we create, distribute and use our money isn't such a big deal when compared to all of the things that have happened to us over the last hundred years. Managing the transition will no doubt present some challenges but they will be insignificant when compared with the troubles that lie in store if we persist with our current dysfunctional system which divides us into hard-hearted creditors and resentful debtors who will inevitably come to blows when the unsustainability of our money creating system reaches its limits and the greed and stupidity that underlies it drives more and more of us into unnecessary poverty. If we don't take the opportunity to change for the better we will soon be overtaken by changes for the worse. The reforms proposed by Positive Money and the Common Cashflow Fund provide a foundation for change on which we can build a better future for us all, thanks to the magic of ***our*** money.

References

Matthew Bishop (2009). *Economics. An A-Z Guide.* London: The Economist/Profile Books Ltd.

Steve Keen (2011). *Debunking Economics – Revised and Expanded Edition: The Naked Emperor Dethroned?* London; New York: Zed Books Ltd.

Josh Ryan-Collins, Tony Greenham, Richard Werner, Andrew Jackson (2011). *Where Does Money Come From? A guide to the UK monetary and banking system.* London: new economics foundation.

Andrew Jackson, Ben Dyson, Graham Hodgson (2013). *The Positive Money System.* London: Positive Money.

Edward Holloway (1981). *How Guernsey Beat The Bankers.* Guernsey: Toucan Press.

Irving Fisher (1933). *Stamp Scrip.* New York: Adelphi.

Bernard Lietaer (2001). *The Future of Money.* London: Random House.

Bank of England (2012, 2013).
http://www.bankofengland.co.uk/statistics/Pages/default.aspx

Office for National Statistics (2012, 2013).
http://www.ons.gov.uk/ons/index.html

Institute for Fiscal Studies (2012, 2013).
http://ifs.org.uk/publications

A Minimum Income Standard for the UK in 2012. Joseph Rowntree Foundation.
http://www.jrf.org.uk/sites/files/jrf/minimum-income-standards-2012-full.pdf

Printed in Great Britain
by Amazon.co.uk, Ltd.,
Marston Gate.